Count by Tens, Fives, and Twos

Connect the dots.
Start at the ▲ and count by tens to 100.
Start at the ● and count by fives to 100.
Start at the ■ and count by twos from 50 to 100.

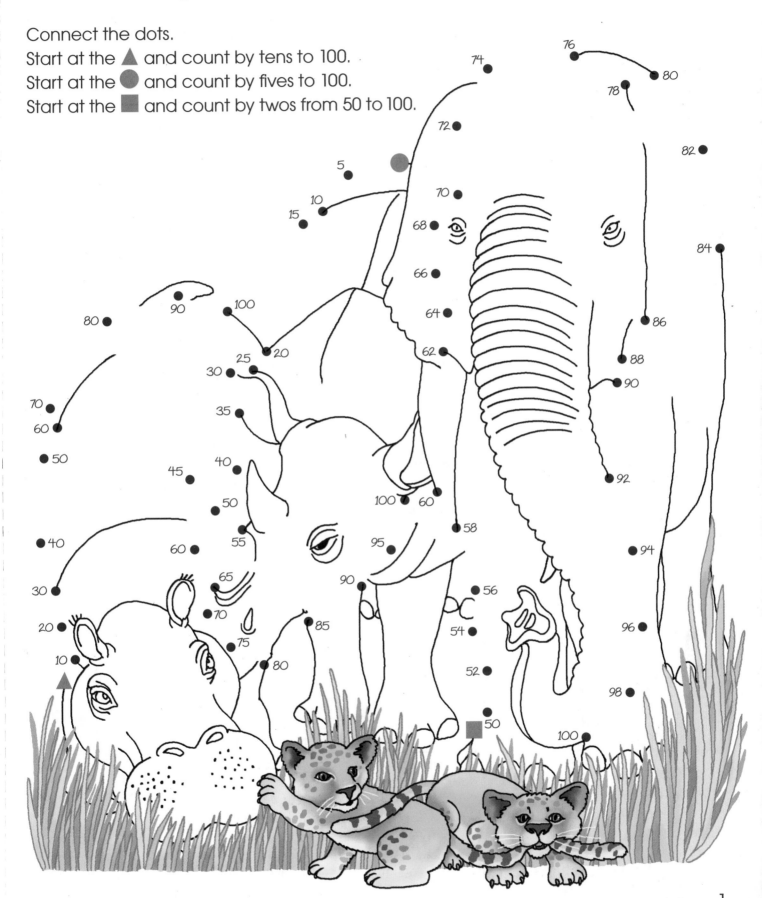

Count to 100

Complete the chart. Count to 100.

1	2			5		7			10
11		13			16		18		
21			24					29	
	32			35					40
		43				47			
51			54				58		
	62					67			70
				75				79	
81					86				
		93						98	100

Count by tens.
Circle the tens.

tens

Count by fives.
Circle the fives.

fives

Count by twos.
Circle the twos.

twos

Challenge: Which types of numbers are always even numbers?

Numbers 1-100; even and odd numbers

Greater or Less

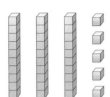 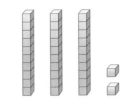

Greater means more than. Less means not as many.

Greater means more than.
Less means not as many.

The symbol points to the number that is less.

35 is **greater** than 32.

35 > 32

or

32 is **less** than 35.

32 < 35

<u>35</u> > <u>32</u>

Write the number for each group. Compare the numbers.
Then write < or > in the ◯.

1.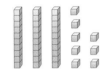

____ ◯ ____

2.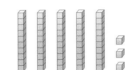

____ ◯ ____

3.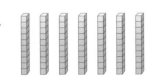

____ ◯ ____

4.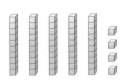

____ ◯ ____

Compare the numbers. Then write < or > in the ◯.

5. 48 ◯ 58   6. 72 ◯ 27   7. 70 ◯ 67

8. 77 ◯ 69   9. 39 ◯ 93   10. 57 ◯ 51

© School Zone Publishing Company   Identify and compare two-digit numbers 3

Numbers in Order

Write the missing numbers.

1. 41, 42, _____, 44, _____, _____, 47, _____, _____, 50

2. 87, _____, 89, _____, 91, _____, _____, 94, _____, 96

3. 66, _____, _____, 69, _____, _____, 72, _____, 74, _____

4. _____, 74, _____, _____, 77, _____, 79, _____, 81, _____

5. _____, _____, 38, _____, _____, 41, _____, _____, 44, _____

Write the numbers in order from **least** to **greatest**.

6. 36, 19, 47, 21   _____, _____, _____, _____

7. 76, 65, 33, 56   _____, _____, _____, _____

8. 59, 46, 32, 17   _____, _____, _____, _____

9. 89, 26, 39, 19   _____, _____, _____, _____

10. 73, 67, 37, 63   _____, _____, _____, _____

Compare and order two-digit numbers

Numbers and Number Names

Number Words to Know

1	one	10	ten
2	two	20	twenty
3	three	30	thirty
4	four	40	forty
5	five	50	fifty
6	six	60	sixty
7	seven	70	seventy
8	eight	80	eighty
9	nine	90	ninety

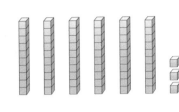

__6__ tens __3__ ones

Number: __63__
Number Name: __sixty-three__

  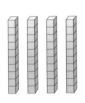   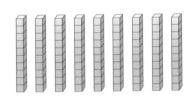

10 ten   20 twenty   30 thirty   40 forty   50 fifty

60 sixty   70 seventy   80 eighty   90 ninety

Write the number of tens and ones.
Then write the number and number name.

1.

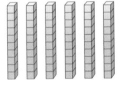

_____ tens _____ ones = _____

_____

2.

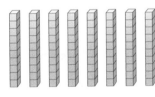

_____ tens _____ ones = _____

_____

3.

_____ tens _____ ones = _____

_____

4.

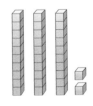

_____ tens _____ ones = _____

_____

More Number Names

More Number Words to Know

Number: _____17_____

Number Name: _____seventeen_____

Write the number.

1. twelve _____

2. sixteen _____

3. fifty _____

4. forty-seven _____

5. eleven _____

6. fifteen _____

Write the number name.

7. 18 _____

8. 70 _____

9. 14 _____

10. 38 _____

11. 56 _____

12. 17 _____

13. 13 _____

14. 93 _____

15. 6 tens _____

16. 19 ones _____

17. 2 tens 9 ones _____

18. 6 tens 8 ones _____

Ordinal Numbers

An **ordinal number** tells the position of an object.

1st	2nd	3rd	4th	5th	6th	7th	8th	9th	10th

first · second · third · fourth · fifth · sixth · seventh · eighth · ninth · tenth

1. Write the ordinal number under each horse.

1st _____ _____ _____ _____ _____

2. Write the ordinal number word under each horse.

seventh _____ _____ _____

Write the ordinal number, child's name, or number in the blank.

3. If Amy is 1st, then Don is _____ . If Bob is 2nd, then Gina is _____ .

4. If Hilary is 8th, how many people are ahead of her? _____

5. If Amy is 1st, then _____ is the 9th person in line.

Challenge: If Katy is 1st, then who is 5th in line? _____

Ordinal numbers: 1st through 10th

More Ordinal Numbers

Here are more **ordinal numbers** to know:

1st	first	10th	tenth	19th	nineteenth	50th	fiftieth
2nd	second	11th	eleventh	20th	twentieth	...	
3rd	third	12th	twelfth	21st	twenty-first	60th	sixtieth
4th	fourth	13th	thirteenth	22nd	twenty-second	...	
5th	fifth	14th	fourteenth	23rd	twenty-third	70th	seventieth
6th	sixth	15th	fifteenth	24th	twenty-fourth	...	
7th	seventh	16th	sixteenth	...		80th	eightieth
8th	eighth	17th	seventeenth	30th	thirtieth	...	
9th	ninth	18th	eighteenth	...		90th	ninetieth
				40th	fortieth	...	
				...		99th	ninety-ninth

Write the ordinal number.

1. fifteenth _____

2. fifth _____

3. fifty-second _____

4. fiftieth _____

5. thirty-fourth _____

6. sixty-third _____

Write the ordinal number word.

7. 11th _____

8. 19th _____

9. 31st _____

10. 43rd _____

11. 29th _____

12. 95th _____

Write the number or ordinal number in the blank.

13. How many children are in front of the 12th child in line? _____

14. If there are 46 children in a line, which number is the next child to come? _____

15. The _____ child is in front of the 60th child in line.

16. The _____ child is 10 places behind the 23rd child in line.

Fact Families

A **fact family** uses the same numbers in its addition and subtraction problems.

$$
\begin{array}{c}
4 \\
+\ 3 \\
\hline
\boxed{7}
\end{array}
\qquad
\begin{array}{c}
\boxed{3} \\
+\ 4 \\
\hline
7
\end{array}
\qquad
\begin{array}{c}
7 \\
-\ 3 \\
\hline
\boxed{4}
\end{array}
\qquad
\begin{array}{c}
\boxed{7} \\
-\ 4 \\
\hline
3
\end{array}
$$

Fill in the missing numbers for each fact family.

1.
$$
\begin{array}{c} 2 \\ +\ 5 \\ \hline \square \end{array}
\quad
\begin{array}{c} 5 \\ +\ \square \\ \hline 7 \end{array}
\quad
\begin{array}{c} 7 \\ -\ 2 \\ \hline \square \end{array}
\quad
\begin{array}{c} \square \\ -\ 5 \\ \hline 2 \end{array}
$$

2.
$$
\begin{array}{c} \square \\ +\ 3 \\ \hline 9 \end{array}
\quad
\begin{array}{c} 3 \\ +\ 6 \\ \hline \square \end{array}
\quad
\begin{array}{c} 9 \\ -\ \square \\ \hline 3 \end{array}
\quad
\begin{array}{c} 9 \\ -\ \square \\ \hline 6 \end{array}
$$

3.
$$
\begin{array}{c} 4 \\ +\ 5 \\ \hline \square \end{array}
\quad
\begin{array}{c} \square \\ +\ 4 \\ \hline 9 \end{array}
\quad
\begin{array}{c} 9 \\ -\ \square \\ \hline 5 \end{array}
\quad
\begin{array}{c} \square \\ -\ 5 \\ \hline 4 \end{array}
$$

4.
$$
\begin{array}{c} 6 \\ +\ \square \\ \hline 6 \end{array}
\quad
\begin{array}{c} 0 \\ +\ \square \\ \hline 6 \end{array}
\quad
\begin{array}{c} 6 \\ -\ \square \\ \hline 0 \end{array}
\quad
\begin{array}{c} 6 \\ -\ \square \\ \hline 6 \end{array}
$$

5.
$$
\begin{array}{c} 6 \\ +\ 7 \\ \hline \square \end{array}
\quad
\begin{array}{c} \square \\ +\ 6 \\ \hline 13 \end{array}
\quad
\begin{array}{c} 13 \\ -\ 7 \\ \hline \square \end{array}
\quad
\begin{array}{c} \square \\ -\ 6 \\ \hline 7 \end{array}
$$

6.
$$
\begin{array}{c} 8 \\ +\ \square \\ \hline 13 \end{array}
\quad
\begin{array}{c} 5 \\ +\ 8 \\ \hline \square \end{array}
\quad
\begin{array}{c} 13 \\ -\ \square \\ \hline 5 \end{array}
\quad
\begin{array}{c} 13 \\ -\ 5 \\ \hline \square \end{array}
$$

7.
$$
\begin{array}{c} 7 \\ +\ 9 \\ \hline \square \end{array}
\quad
\begin{array}{c} \square \\ +\ 7 \\ \hline 16 \end{array}
\quad
\begin{array}{c} 16 \\ -\ 9 \\ \hline \square \end{array}
\quad
\begin{array}{c} \square \\ -\ 7 \\ \hline 9 \end{array}
$$

8.
$$
\begin{array}{c} 4 \\ +\ \square \\ \hline 12 \end{array}
\quad
\begin{array}{c} 8 \\ +\ 4 \\ \hline \square \end{array}
\quad
\begin{array}{c} 12 \\ -\ \square \\ \hline 4 \end{array}
\quad
\begin{array}{c} 12 \\ -\ \square \\ \hline 8 \end{array}
$$

More Fact Families

All of the number sentences in a **fact family** use the same numbers.

3, 9, 12

$3 + 9 = 12$
$9 + 3 = 12$
$12 - 3 = 9$
$12 - 9 = 3$

Write the addition and subtraction facts for each family.

1.　6, 8, 14

_____

_____

_____

_____

2.　4, 9, 13

_____

_____

_____

_____

3.　7, 8, 15

_____

_____

_____

_____

4.　5, 7, 12

_____

_____

_____

_____

5.　5, 9, 14

_____

_____

_____

_____

6.　8, 9, 17

_____

_____

_____

_____

7.　6, 9, 15

_____

_____

_____

_____

8.　9, 0, 9

_____

_____

_____

_____

9.　7, 7, 14

_____

_____

_____

Fast Facts!

Watch the signs!

Time yourself. Can you do all of these problems in less than 5 minutes?

1. 2 + 5 = ____	13. 6 – 2 = ____	25. 3 + 7 = ____	37. 12 – 6 = ____
2. 4 + 0 = ____	14. 7 + 6 = ____	26. 15 – 9 = ____	38. 2 + 9 = ____
3. 9 – 1 = ____	15. 12 – 7 = ____	27. 5 + 9 = ____	39. 9 + 7 = ____
4. 5 + 8 = ____	16. 11 – 4 = ____	28. 8 – 2 = ____	40. 7 + 8 = ____
5. 13 – 4 = ____	17. 8 – 1 = ____	29. 7 + 5 = ____	41. 10 – 1 = ____
6. 5 + 6 = ____	18. 2 + 9 = ____	30. 13 – 8 = ____	42. 3 + 6 = ____
7. 15 – 7 = ____	19. 4 + 8 = ____	31. 9 – 0 = ____	43. 9 + 9 = ____
8. 9 + 5 = ____	20. 7 – 0 = ____	32. 8 + 8 = ____	44. 13 – 7 = ____
9. 4 – 4 = ____	21. 6 + 9 = ____	33. 12 – 3 = ____	45. 4 + 6 = ____
10. 16 – 9 = ____	22. 14 – 8 = ____	34. 9 + 8 = ____	46. 11 – 5 = ____
11. 9 + 0 = ____	23. 2 + 6 = ____	35. 6 + 8 = ____	47. 17 – 8 = ____
12. 14 – 7 = ____	24. 12 – 4 = ____	36. 11 – 3 = ____	48. 9 + 5 = ____

Addition Properties

```
  6
  3
+ 4
─────
 13
```

To make adding easier, look for "tens".
You can add numbers in any order.
$6 + 4 = 10$, then $10 + 3 = 13$.

Addition properties are rules for addition that are always true.
Here are some addition properties to know:

Commutative Property of Addition	**Associative Property of Addition**	**Identity Property of Addition**
Changing the **order** of the addends does not change the sum.	Changing the **grouping** of the addends does not change the sum.	The sum of any number and **zero** is that same number.
$5 + 2 = 2 + 5$	$(5 + 2) + 3 = 5 + (2 + 3)$	$7 + 0 = 7$
$7 = 7$	$10 = 10$	

Write the sum or missing addend.

1.
```
  7
  5
+ 3
───
```
2.
```
  8
  0
+ 7
───
```
3.
```
  9
  2
+ 8
───
```
4.
```
  6
  5
+ 4
───
```
5.
```
  7
  7
+ 3
───
```

6.
```
  4
  5
  2
+ 6
───
```
7.
```
  2
  0
  3
+ 8
───
```
8.
```
  3
  5
  4
+ 7
───
```
9.
```
  4
  4
  2
+ 2
───
```
10.
```
  9
  3
  1
+ 5
───
```

11. $5 + 7 + 5 = \underline{\hspace{2cm}}$

12. $6 + 0 + (4 + 7) = \underline{\hspace{2cm}}$

13. $(3 + 2) + 7 = \underline{\hspace{2cm}}$

14. $5 + 6 + 5 + 3 = \underline{\hspace{2cm}}$

15. $4 + 3 + \underline{\hspace{1.5cm}} = 14$

16. $(6 + \underline{\hspace{1.5cm}}) + (2 + 2) = 10$

17. $(8 + 1) + \underline{\hspace{1.5cm}} = 9$

18. $4 + 3 + 2 + \underline{\hspace{1.5cm}} = 10$

Add Two-Digit Numbers

Add the **ones**.
Regroup as needed.

$$\begin{array}{r} {}^{1} \\ 3\,6 \\ +\ 5\,9 \\ \hline 5 \end{array}$$

6 + 9 = **15 ones**
15 ones is
1 ten and **5 ones**.

Add the **tens**.

$$\begin{array}{r} {}^{1} \\ 3\,6 \\ +\ 5\,9 \\ \hline 9\,5 \end{array}$$

1 + 3 + 5 = **9 tens**
The **sum** is **95**.

Check:

$$\begin{array}{r} {}^{1} \\ 5\,9 \\ +\ 3\,6 \\ \hline 9\,5 \end{array}$$

Add the numbers
in a different order
to check your answer.

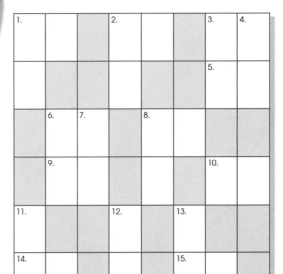

Find the sums to fill in the puzzle.

Across

1. $\begin{array}{r} 55 \\ +\ 37 \\ \hline \end{array}$
2. $\begin{array}{r} 29 \\ +\ 46 \\ \hline \end{array}$
3. $\begin{array}{r} 47 \\ +\ 18 \\ \hline \end{array}$
5. $\begin{array}{r} 18 \\ +\ 15 \\ \hline \end{array}$
6. $\begin{array}{r} 59 \\ +\ 17 \\ \hline \end{array}$
8. $\begin{array}{r} 77 \\ +\ 15 \\ \hline \end{array}$

9. $\begin{array}{r} 25 \\ +\ 18 \\ \hline \end{array}$
10. $\begin{array}{r} 24 \\ +\ 67 \\ \hline \end{array}$

14. $\begin{array}{r} 14 \\ +\ 19 \\ \hline \end{array}$
15. $\begin{array}{r} 35 \\ +\ 16 \\ \hline \end{array}$

Down

1. $\begin{array}{r} 28 \\ +\ 68 \\ \hline \end{array}$
2. $\begin{array}{r} 39 \\ +\ 35 \\ \hline \end{array}$
3. $\begin{array}{r} 24 \\ +\ 39 \\ \hline \end{array}$
4. $\begin{array}{r} 17 \\ +\ 36 \\ \hline \end{array}$

6. $\begin{array}{r} 28 \\ +\ 46 \\ \hline \end{array}$
7. $\begin{array}{r} 34 \\ +\ 29 \\ \hline \end{array}$
8. $\begin{array}{r} 76 \\ +\ 14 \\ \hline \end{array}$
11. $\begin{array}{r} 45 \\ +\ 38 \\ \hline \end{array}$
12. $\begin{array}{r} 37 \\ +\ 58 \\ \hline \end{array}$
13. $\begin{array}{r} 29 \\ +\ 36 \\ \hline \end{array}$

Add Three or More Numbers

Add: 32 + 8 + 14

Add the **ones**.
Regroup as needed.

```
  ¹
 3 2
   8
+ 1 4
─────
   4
```

2 + 8 + 4 = **14 ones**
14 ones is **1 ten**
and **4 ones**.

Add the **tens**.

```
  ¹
 3 2
   8
+ 1 4
─────
 5 4
```

1 + 3 + 1 = **5 tens**
The **sum** is **54**.

Check:

```
  ¹
 1 4
   8
+ 3 2
─────
 5 4
```

Write the sum.

1.
```
  32
   7
+ 20
────
```

2.
```
  18
   1
+ 36
────
```

3.
```
  21
   0
+  3
────
```

4.
```
  76
   2
+ 11
────
```

5.
```
   2
  18
+  5
────
```

6.
```
  51
   5
+  2
────
```

7.
```
   8
  27
+  9
────
```

8.
```
  32
  22
+  5
────
```

9.
```
  56
  33
+ 10
────
```

10.
```
  35
  42
+  5
────
```

11.
```
  25
   3
  21
+  5
────
```

12.
```
  19
  25
  46
+ 14
────
```

13.
```
  62
  70
   2
+ 54
────
```

14.
```
  62
   8
  33
+  5
────
```

15.
```
  83
   5
  20
+  9
────
```

Write the sum. Use the space below to show your work.

16. 53 + 6 + 24 = _____

17. 39 + 23 + 4 + 33= _____

18. 16 + 30 + 9 + 21 = _____

Subtract Two-Digit Numbers

Subtract the **ones**.
Regroup as needed.

```
  3 2
- 1 9
─────
  ?
```

2–9 cannot be done.
You must regroup. **3 tens**
and **2 ones** is the same as
2 tens and **12 ones**.

Regroup.
Subtract the **ones**.

```
  ²3̸ ¹²2̸
-   1 9
─────
      3
```

12 – 9 = 3 **ones**

Subtract the **tens**.

```
  ²3̸ ¹²2̸
-   1 9
─────
  1 3
```

2 – 1 = 1 **ten**
The **difference** is 13.

Check:

```
  ¹
  1 3
+ 1 9
─────
  3 2
```

Add to check
your answer.

Write the difference.

1.
```
  65
- 22
────
```

2.
```
  28
- 13
────
```

3.
```
  63
- 24
────
```

4.
```
  96
- 35
────
```

5.
```
  86
- 85
────
```

6.
```
  78
- 33
────
```

7.
```
  36
- 28
────
```

8.
```
  77
- 35
────
```

9.
```
  80
- 31
────
```

10.
```
  92
- 54
────
```

11.
```
  67
- 18
────
```

12.
```
  36
- 27
────
```

13.
```
  99
- 44
────
```

14.
```
  85
- 49
────
```

15.
```
  82
- 55
────
```

16.
```
  90
- 25
────
```

The answer to a subtraction
problem is called the **difference**.

Add and Subtract Two-Digit Numbers

Solve this riddle:

What is the largest land animal?

Add and subtract to find the answer.

A	B	C	E	F
73 + 17	82 − 17	18 + 33	80 − 34	79 − 19

H	I	L	N	P
70 − 25	88 − 79	14 + 36	91 − 15	93 − 18

R	S	T	U	A
69 + 26	79 + 19	73 − 17	82 + 17	27 18 + 45

E	H	N	A
28 + 18	19 + 26	19 25 + 32	67 + 23

The ＿＿ ＿＿ ＿＿ ＿＿ ＿＿ ＿＿ ＿＿
   90   60   95   9   51   90   76

＿＿ ＿＿ ＿＿ ＿＿   ＿＿ ＿＿ ＿＿ ＿＿ ＿＿ ＿＿ ＿＿ ＿＿
65 99 98 45   46 50 46 75 45 90 76 56

Column Addition and Subtraction

Rewrite the problem in vertical form. Then find the sum or difference.

1. $52 + 24$	2. $79 - 17$	3. $43 + 18$	4. $86 - 68$	5. $48 + 40$
6. $75 - 39$	7. $57 + 23$	8. $90 - 37$	9. $76 + 20$	10. $45 + 9 + 23$
11. $64 + 9$	12. $73 - 8$	13. $39 + 19$	14. $50 - 42$	15. $9 + 23 + 49$
16. $87 - 79$	17. $45 + 35$	18. $63 + 29$	19. $91 - 45$	20. $60 - 18$

Add and subtract one-digit and two-digit numbers

Add or Subtract to Solve Problems

Jason found 18 starfish on the beach. Jose found 14 starfish, and Jay found 6 starfish. How many more starfish did Jason find than Jose?

Use these 4 steps to help you solve word problems:

1. **Read** the problem carefully.
2. **Decide** what to do.
3. **Solve** the problem.
4. **Check** to see if the answer makes sense.

Read: Which boys is the question asking about? Which numbers do you use?

Decide: add or (subtract)

Solve:
$$\begin{array}{r} 18 \\ -14 \\ \hline 4 \end{array} \text{ starfish}$$

Check: 18 is 4 more than 14.

Read the problem. Circle add or subtract. Solve the problem. Label your answer.

1. Kayla, Sara, and Maria are at the beach. Kayla found 17 shells, Sara found 46 shells, and Maria found 23 shells. How many shells did they find altogether?

   add or **subtract** _____

2. Kayla, Sara, and Maria are at the beach. Kayla found 17 shells, Sara found 46 shells, and Maria found 23 shells. Sara sold 28 shells. How many shells does Sara have left?

   add or **subtract** _____

3. Jason found 18 starfish on the beach. Jose found 14 starfish, and Jay found 46 starfish. How many starfish did Jose and Jay find?

   add or **subtract** _____

4. Jason found 18 starfish on the beach. Jose found 14 starfish, and Jay found 6 starfish. How many more starfish does Jose have than Jay?

   add or **subtract** _____

Round Two-Digit Numbers

To **round** a number to the **nearest ten**, look at the **ones** place.
If the digit in the ones place is **5 or more**, then **round up**.
If the digit in the ones place is **4 or less**, then **round down**.

Is 83 closer to 80 or 90? _80_

Round 83 to 80.

```
90
89
88
87
86  ↑
85  │
84  ┐
83  │ ↓
82
81
80
```

Look at the boldface number. To round, circle the nearest ten.

1. **32**	30	40	2. **89**	80	90
3. **19**	10	20	4. **64**	60	70
5. **55**	50	60	6. **26**	20	30
7. **41**	40	50	8. **77**	70	80
9. **28**	20	30	10. **39**	30	40
11. **62**	60	70	12. **33**	30	40

Round the number to the nearest ten.

13. 64 _____	14. 86 _____
15. 22 _____	16. 49 _____
17. 31 _____	18. 43 _____
19. 35 _____	20. 67 _____
21. 18 _____	22. 13 _____
23. 89 _____	24. 76 _____

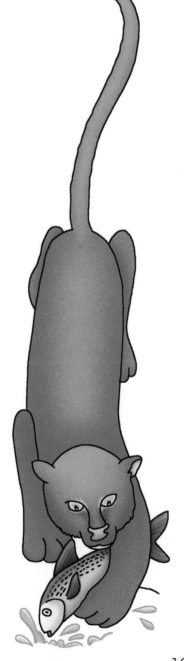

Estimate Sums and Differences

Estimate the sums and differences by **rounding** to the **nearest ten.**

Estimate the sum.

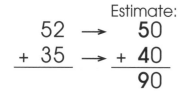

```
            Estimate:
  52  →      50
+ 35  →    + 40
            90
```

Estimate the difference.

```
            Estimate:
  71  →      70
- 35  →    - 40
            30
```

Round the numbers to the nearest ten.
Write the estimate for the sum or difference.

1.
```
              Estimate:
  17   →     _____

+ 22   →   + _____

           _____
```

2.
```
              Estimate:
  65   →     _____

- 19   →   - _____

           _____
```

3.
```
              Estimate:
  75   →     _____

- 47   →   - _____

           _____
```

4.
```
              Estimate:
  53   →     _____

+ 29   →   + _____

           _____
```

Estimate the sum or difference.

5. 46 + 38 _____

6. 81 – 29 _____

7. 46 – 38 _____

8. 43 + 25 _____

9. 83 + 12 _____

10. 83 – 12 _____

Hundreds, Tens, and Ones

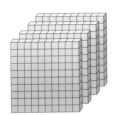

__4__ hundreds __5__ tens __7__ ones

$400 + 50 + 7$

457

Look at the picture. Count how many hundreds, tens, and ones there are.
Then write the number.

1.

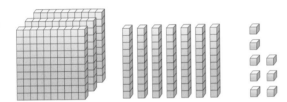

_____ hundreds _____ tens _____ ones

_____ + _____ + _____

_____

2.

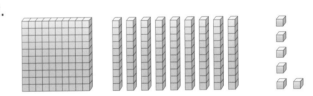

_____ hundreds _____ tens _____ ones

_____ + _____ + _____

_____

3.

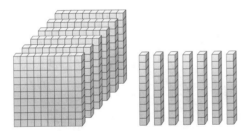

_____ hundreds _____ tens _____ ones

_____ + _____ + _____

_____

4.

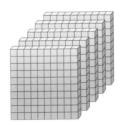

_____ hundreds _____ tens _____ ones

_____ + _____ + _____

_____

Expanded Notation

Write the number in **expanded notation** using **words**.

372 = **3** hundreds + **7** tens + **2** ones

Write the number in **expanded notation** using **digits**.

372 = 300 + 70 + 2

Write the number in expanded notation using words.

1. 749 = _____ + _____ + _____

2. 514 = _____ + _____ + _____

3. 930 = _____ + _____ + _____

4. 398 = _____ + _____ + _____

5. 607 = _____ + _____ + _____

Write the number in expanded notation using digits.

6. 562 = _____ + _____ + _____

7. 953 = _____ + _____ + _____

8. 370 = _____ + _____ + _____

9. 617 = _____ + _____ + _____

10. 109 = _____ + _____ + _____

Number Names

Writing three-digit numbers in expanded notation can help you write their number names.

437 = <u>4 hundreds + 3 tens + 7 ones</u>   609 = <u>6 hundreds + 9 ones</u>   140 = <u>1 hundred + 4 tens</u>

437 = four hundred thirty-seven   609 = six hundred nine   140 = one hundred forty

---

Write the number in expanded notation. Then write the number name.

1. 592 = _____ + _____ + _____

   592 = _____

2. 106 = _____ + _____ + _____

   106 = _____

3. 820 = _____ + _____ + _____

   820 = _____

Write the number name.

4. 372 = _____

5. 189 = _____

6. 601 = _____

7. 715 = _____

8. 280 = _____

Write the number.

9. three hundred six = _____

10. nine hundred nineteen = _____

11. four hundred eighty-two = _____

12. one hundred ninety-seven = _____

13. five hundred fifty = _____

14. eight hundred twelve = _____

Place Value

hundreds tens ones

$$538 = 5 \quad 3 \quad 8$$

Circle the correct digit in the number.

1. Circle the tens.   4 5 3

2. Circle the hundreds.   7 4 6

3. Circle the ones.   1 6 8

4. Circle the hundreds.   3 9 1

5. Circle the tens.   2 1 0

6. Circle the ones.   7 6 5

Circle the correct number.

7. Which number shows 4 tens?   374   347   473

8. Which number shows 6 hundreds?   605   506   560

9. Which number shows 9 ones?   981   891   819

10. Which number shows 7 hundreds?   275   527   725

11. Which number shows 0 tens?   460   406   640

12. Which number shows 3 hundreds?   543   435   345

Challenge: Make as many three-digit numbers as you can using the digits 4, 6, and 9.

Greater or Less

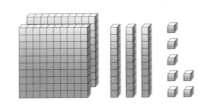

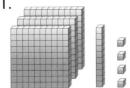

246 > 237

The symbol points to the number that is less.

246 is **greater** than 237.
246 > 237
or
237 is **less** than 246.
237 < 246

Write the number for each group. Compare the numbers.
Then write < or > in the ⬤ .

1.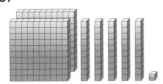

_____ ⬤ _____

2.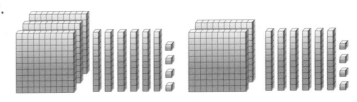

_____ ⬤ _____

3.

_____ ⬤ _____

4.

_____ ⬤ _____

Compare the numbers. Then write < or > in the ⬤ .

5. 438 ⬤ 538   6. 572 ⬤ 527   7. 706 ⬤ 670

8. 717 ⬤ 619   9. 390 ⬤ 930   10. 537 ⬤ 573

Identify and compare three-digit numbers

Numbers in Order

Write the missing numbers.

1. 111,_____,113, _____, _____, 116, _____, _____,119, _____

2. 307,_____,309,_____, 311,_____, _____, 314, _____, 316

3. 555,_____, _____,558,_____, _____, 561,_____, 563,_____

4. 710, 720,_____,740,_____, 760, _____, _____,790,_____

5. 872, 874,_____, 878,_____, 882,_____, _____, 888,_____

Write the numbers in order from **least** to **greatest**.

6. 319, 721, 976, 351   _____, _____, _____, _____

7. 572, 897, 711, 999   _____, _____, _____, _____

8. 702, 724, 237, 700   _____, _____, _____, _____

9. 808, 788, 896, 418   _____, _____, _____, _____

10. 987, 813, 381, 789   _____, _____, _____, _____

Count by Hundreds, Tens, and Ones

Connect the dots.
Start at the ▲ and count by hundreds to 900.
Start at the ● and count by tens from 510 to 600.
Start at the ■ and count by ones from 375 to 390.

Greater or Less

345, 354, 435, 453 < 500

Find and write all the three-digit numbers that make the sentence true.

1.

_____ < 400

2.

_____ < 600

3.

_____ < 450

4.

_____ < 550

5.

_____ < 700

6.

_____ < 650

Round Three-Digit Numbers

To **round** a number to the **nearest hundred**, look at the **tens** place.
If the digit in the tens place is **5 or more**, then **round up**.
If the digit in the tens place is **4 or less**, then **round down**.

Is 235 closer to 200 or 300?

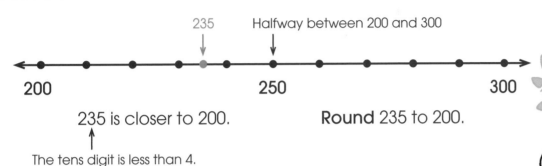

235
Halfway between 200 and 300

200   250   300

235 is closer to 200.   **Round** 235 to 200.

The tens digit is less than 4.

Look at the boldface number. To round, circle the nearest hundred.

1. **479**	400	500	2. **716**	700	800	3. **647**	600	700
4. **328**	300	400	5. **761**	700	800	6. **153**	100	200
7. **505**	500	600	8. **350**	300	400	9. **808**	800	900

Round the number to the nearest hundred.

10. 347 _____   11. 609 _____   12. 178 _____

13. 307 _____   14. 649 _____   15. 595 _____

16. 370 _____   17. 469 _____   18. 350 _____

Round the number to the nearest ten.

19. 138   *140*   20. 246 _____

21. 672 _____   22. 472 _____

23. 485 _____   24. 555 _____

Do you remember how to round numbers to the nearest ten? Look at the ones digit.

Estimate Sums and Differences

Estimate the sums and differences by **rounding** to the **nearest hundred**.

Estimate the sum.

		Estimate:
527	→	500
+ 354	→	+ 400
		900

Estimate the difference.

		Estimate:
718	→	700
– 345	→	– 300
		400

Round the numbers to the nearest hundred.
Write the estimate for the sum or difference.

Estimate:

1. 671 → _____

   + 238 → + _____

   _____

Estimate:

2. 650 → _____

   – 109 → – _____

   _____

Estimate:

3. 475 → _____

   – 147 → – _____

   _____

Estimate:

4. 535 → _____

   + 259 → + _____

   _____

Estimate the sum or difference.

5. 246 + 381 _____

6. 815 – 209 _____

7. 466 – 308 _____

8. 463 + 295 _____

9. 809 + 95 _____

10. 853 – 8 _____

Add Three-Digit Numbers

Add the ones.
Regroup as needed.

$$\begin{array}{r} 3\overset{1}{4}6 \\ + 286 \\ \hline 2 \end{array}$$

6 + 6 = **12 ones**
12 ones is
1 ten and **2 ones**.

Add the tens.
Regroup as needed.

$$\begin{array}{r} \overset{1}{3}\overset{1}{4}6 \\ + 286 \\ \hline 32 \end{array}$$

1 + 4 + 8 = **13 tens**
13 tens is
1 hundred and **3 tens**.

Add the hundreds.

$$\begin{array}{r} \overset{1}{3}\overset{1}{4}6 \\ + 286 \\ \hline 632 \end{array}$$

1 + 3 + 2 = **6 hundreds**
The **sum** is **632**.

Estimate:

$$\begin{array}{r} 300 \\ + 300 \\ \hline 600 \end{array}$$

Write the sum.

1. $\begin{array}{r} 221 \\ + 579 \\ \hline \end{array}$
2. $\begin{array}{r} 398 \\ + 352 \\ \hline \end{array}$
3. $\begin{array}{r} 375 \\ + 246 \\ \hline \end{array}$
4. $\begin{array}{r} 200 \\ + 200 \\ \hline \end{array}$

5. $\begin{array}{r} 519 \\ + 399 \\ \hline \end{array}$
6. $\begin{array}{r} 600 \\ + 300 \\ \hline \end{array}$
7. $\begin{array}{r} 634 \\ + 200 \\ \hline \end{array}$
8. $\begin{array}{r} 721 \\ + 189 \\ \hline \end{array}$

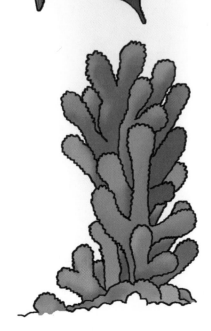

9. $\begin{array}{r} 496 \\ + 366 \\ \hline \end{array}$
10. $\begin{array}{r} 100 \\ + 500 \\ \hline \end{array}$
11. $\begin{array}{r} 519 \\ + 181 \\ \hline \end{array}$
12. $\begin{array}{r} 131 \\ + 689 \\ \hline \end{array}$

13. $\begin{array}{r} 700 \\ + 197 \\ \hline \end{array}$
14. $\begin{array}{r} 400 \\ + 450 \\ \hline \end{array}$
15. $\begin{array}{r} 647 \\ + 188 \\ \hline \end{array}$
16. $\begin{array}{r} 200 \\ + 600 \\ \hline \end{array}$

Add Three or More Numbers

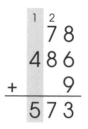

Add: 78 + 486 + 9

Add the **ones**. Regroup as needed.	Add the **tens**. Regroup as needed.	Add the **hundreds**.	Estimate:
$\overset{2}{7}8$ 486 + 9 ——— 3	$\overset{1}{7}\overset{2}{8}$ 486 + 9 ——— 73	$\overset{1}{7}\overset{2}{8}$ 486 + 9 ——— 573	100 500 + 0 ——— 600
8 + 6 + 9 = **23 ones** **23 ones** is **2 tens** and **3 ones**.	2 + 7 + 8 = **17 tens** **17 tens** is **1 hundred** and **7 tens**.	1 + 4 = **5 hundreds** The **sum** is **573**.	

Write the sum.

1. 132
   206
   + 321

2. 375
   132
   + 81

3. 444
   44
   + 4

4. 506
   56
   + 6

5. 375
   86
   + 409

6. 514
   8
   + 73

7. 193
   45
   + 6

8. 765
   8
   + 43

9. 140
   48
   + 186

10. 349
    79
    + 9

11. 231
    52
    5
    + 111

12. 735
    8
    63
    + 106

13. 321
    232
    175
    + 109

14. 9
    87
    654
    + 123

15. 298
    197
    396
    + 95

Write the sum. Use the space below to show your work.

16. 9 + 65 + 432 = _____   17. 777 + 7 + 77 = _____   18. 325 + 46 + 9 + 555 = _____

Subtract Three-Digit Numbers

Subtract the ones.
Regroup as needed.

$$\begin{array}{r} {}^0\cancel{6}\,{}^{18}\cancel{8} \\ -\ 2\ 0\ 9 \\ \hline 9 \end{array}$$

Regroup 1 ten and 8 ones to 0 tens and 18 ones.
18 – 9 = **9 ones**

Subtract the tens.
Regroup as needed.

$$\begin{array}{r} 6\,{}^0\cancel{7}\,{}^{18}\cancel{8} \\ -\ 2\ 0\ 9 \\ \hline 0\ 9 \end{array}$$

0 – 0 = **0 tens**

Subtract the hundreds.

$$\begin{array}{r} {}^0\cancel{6}\,{}^{18}\cancel{8} \\ -\ 2\ 0\ 9 \\ \hline 4\ 0\ 9 \end{array}$$

6 – 2 = **4 hundreds**
The **difference** is **409**.

Check:

$$\begin{array}{r} {}^1 4\ 0\ 9 \\ +\ 2\ 0\ 9 \\ \hline 6\ 1\ 8 \end{array}$$

Add to check your answer.

Write the difference.

1.
$$\begin{array}{r} 248 \\ -\ 136 \\ \hline \end{array}$$

2.
$$\begin{array}{r} 274 \\ -\ 143 \\ \hline \end{array}$$

3.
$$\begin{array}{r} 343 \\ -\ 133 \\ \hline \end{array}$$

4.
$$\begin{array}{r} 455 \\ -\ 248 \\ \hline \end{array}$$

5.
$$\begin{array}{r} 353 \\ -\ 205 \\ \hline \end{array}$$

6.
$$\begin{array}{r} 326 \\ -\ 250 \\ \hline \end{array}$$

7.
$$\begin{array}{r} 870 \\ -\ 328 \\ \hline \end{array}$$

8.
$$\begin{array}{r} 258 \\ -\ 196 \\ \hline \end{array}$$

9.
$$\begin{array}{r} 694 \\ -\ 589 \\ \hline \end{array}$$

10.
$$\begin{array}{r} 786 \\ -\ 579 \\ \hline \end{array}$$

11.
$$\begin{array}{r} 971 \\ -\ 226 \\ \hline \end{array}$$

12.
$$\begin{array}{r} 777 \\ -\ 456 \\ \hline \end{array}$$

13.
$$\begin{array}{r} 219 \\ -\ 174 \\ \hline \end{array}$$

14.
$$\begin{array}{r} 493 \\ -\ 188 \\ \hline \end{array}$$

15.
$$\begin{array}{r} 800 \\ -\ 250 \\ \hline \end{array}$$

16.
$$\begin{array}{r} 550 \\ -\ 315 \\ \hline \end{array}$$

Subtract Across Zero

Subtract the ones.
Regroup as needed.

$$
\begin{array}{r}
\overset{4}{\cancel{5}}\overset{9}{\cancel{0}}\overset{14}{\cancel{4}} \\
-\ 2\ 4\ 9 \\
\hline
5
\end{array}
$$

You cannot regroup **0 tens**. You must regroup the 5 hundreds to 4 hundreds and 10 tens. Then regroup the 10 tens to 9 tens and 14 ones.
14 – 9 = **5 ones**

Subtract the tens.
Regroup as needed.

$$
\begin{array}{r}
\overset{4}{\cancel{5}}\overset{9}{\cancel{0}}\overset{14}{\cancel{4}} \\
-\ 2\ 4\ 9 \\
\hline
5\ 5
\end{array}
$$

9 – 4 = **5 tens**

Subtract the hundreds.

$$
\begin{array}{r}
\overset{4}{\cancel{5}}\overset{9}{\cancel{0}}\overset{14}{\cancel{4}} \\
-\ 2\ 4\ 9 \\
\hline
2\ 5\ 5
\end{array}
$$

4 – 2 = **2 hundreds**
The **difference** is 255.

Check:

$$
\begin{array}{r}
\overset{1}{\ }\overset{1}{2}\ 5\ 5 \\
+\ 2\ 4\ 9 \\
\hline
5\ 0\ 4
\end{array}
$$

Add to check your answer.

Write the difference.

1. 305
   – 127

2. 702
   – 395

3. 301
   – 106

4. 500
   – 275

5. 403
   – 129

6. 208
   – 159

7. 805
   – 456

8. 900
   – 499

9. 707
   – 358

10. 503
    – 469

11. 301
    – 294

12. 604
    – 406

13. 500
    – 234

14. 706
    – 669

15. 403
    – 388

16. 203
    – 108

Add and Subtract Three-Digit Numbers

Solve this riddle:

What is the largest reptile?

Add and subtract to find the answer.

A	C	D	E	I
476	536	851	741	567
+ 309	+ 164	– 333	– 423	+ 321

L	O	R	S	T
820	626	987	858	409
– 135	+ 259	– 569	– 273	+ 209

W	A	C	E	L
567	907	853	102	246
+ 233	– 122	– 153	106	119
			+ 110	158
				+ 162

O	R	T
742	219	740
+ 143	+ 199	– 122

The ‾585‾ ‾785‾ ‾685‾ ‾618‾ ‾800‾ ‾785‾ ‾618‾ ‾318‾ ‾418‾

‾700‾ ‾418‾ ‾885‾ ‾700‾ ‾885‾ ‾518‾ ‾888‾ ‾685‾ ‾318‾

Puzzle Practice

Find the sum, difference, or number to fill in the puzzle.

Across

1. 362
    + 177

3. 456
    − 225

6. 881
    − 777

7. 436
    + 193

9. 263
    + 388

11. 508
    − 416

12. 836
    − 798

13. 690
    − 123

Down

1. five hundred forty-six _____

2. 563 + 346 = _____

3. 753 − 537 = _____

4. 176 + 129 = _____

5. 706 − 565 = _____

8. two hundred twelve _____

10. seven hundred six _____

11. 903 − 808 = _____

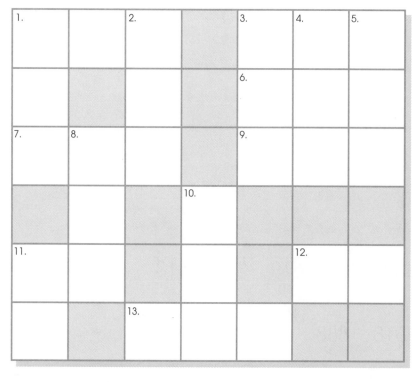

Add and subtract three-digit numbers; three-digit number names

Add or Subtract to Solve Problems

Use these 4 steps to help
you solve word problems:

1. **Read** the problem carefully.
2. **Decide** what to do.
3. **Solve** the problem.
4. **Check** to see if the answer
   makes sense.

Read the problem. Solve the problem.
Show your work. Label your answer.

1. Kevin collected 132 baseball cards
   and 78 football cards over the past
   few years. How many sports cards
   does he have in all?

2. Jesse collects marbles. 257 marbles are
   red, 183 marbles are blue, and
   304 marbles are clear. How many more
   clear marbles does he have than red?

3. Kyra collects buttons. She has
   415 buttons with two holes and
   229 buttons with four holes. Which
   type of button does she have
   more of? How many more?

4. Milo collects stamps from different
   countries. He sorts them by continents.
   He has 45 stamps from Europe, 28 stamps
   from Asia, 9 stamps from Africa, and
   13 stamps from South America. How
   many stamps does he have in all?

5. Ashley is collecting used cans to
   raise money for a charity. In the last
   three weeks, she has collected:
   179 cans the first week, 301 cans the
   second week, and 98 cans the third
   week. How many cans has she
   collected so far?

6. Ashley's goal is to collect 800 used
   cans in a month. Using the answer
   from problem 5, how many more cans
   must she collect in the fourth week to
   meet her goal?

Add or Subtract to Solve Problems

Read the problem. Solve the problem.
Show your work. Label your answer.

1. Laura is reading a book that has
   392 pages. She has already read
   158 pages. How many more pages
   does she have left to read?

2. Jason is putting together a 500-piece
   jigsaw puzzle. He has already used
   347 pieces to complete the puzzle.
   How many pieces are left to complete
   the whole puzzle?

3. Elaine took 173 pictures on Monday
   and 68 pictures on Tuesday. How
   many pictures did she take in all?

4. Matt's family is driving to a city in
   Florida that is 512 miles away. They have
   traveled 309 miles so far. How many
   more miles must they drive to reach
   the city in Florida?

5. There are 365 days in a year.
   How many days are after the
   147th day of the year?

6. On a family road trip, Jack counted
   351 stop signs, 23 yield signs, and
   76 speed limit signs. How many
   more stop signs did he see than
   speed limit signs?

Maps

This map shows distances in miles between some cities in Kansas.

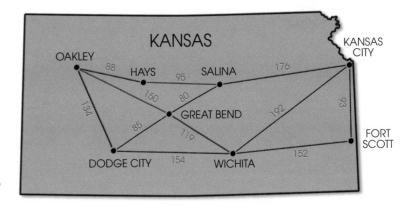

Read the problem. Solve the problem. Show your work. Label your answer.

1. How many miles is it from Fort Scott to Dodge City if you drive through Wichita?

2. How many miles is it from Oakley to Kansas City if you drive through Hays and Salina?

3. Which city is farther from Kansas City, Salina or Wichita? How much farther is it?

4. How far is it from Kansas City to Dodge City if you drive through Fort Scott and Wichita?

5. Which distance is longer, from Kansas City to Dodge City driving through Wichita or from Kansas City to Oakley driving through Salina and Hays? How much longer is it?

6. Find the shortest route between Wichita and Oakley. What is this distance?

Add and subtract to solve word problems; use a map   39

Maps

This map shows distances in miles between some cities in Nevada.

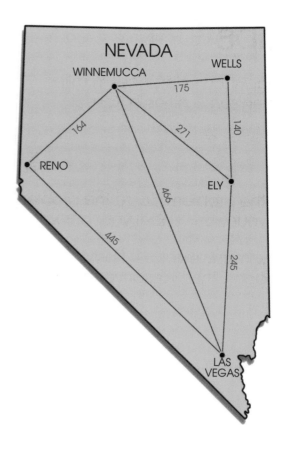

Read the problem. Solve the problem. Show your work. Label your answer.

1. How much farther is it from Las Vegas to Winnemucca than from Las Vegas to Reno?

2. How many miles is it from Wells to Las Vegas if you drive through Ely?

3. How many miles is it from Reno to Wells if you drive through Winnemucca?

4. Which distance is shorter, Reno to Wells or Reno to Ely taking any of the routes shown on the map? How much shorter is it?

5. How far is it if you drive around the state starting and ending in Reno?

Tables

A **table** can be used to show a collection of data. A table uses words and numbers. You have to read a table carefully across and down to find the data you are looking for.

This table shows how many people like different types of fruit.

Favorite Fruit	
Type of Fruit	Number of Votes
Apple	23
Banana	28
Grapes	17
Orange	19

Use the table to answer the questions. Label your answers.

1. How many children voted for grapes? _____

2. How many children voted for apples? _____

3. Which fruit is the favorite? _____

4. Which fruit is the least favorite? _____

5. How many children voted for apples and oranges? _____

6. More children voted for bananas than grapes.
   How many more children voted for bananas? _____

7. About how many children were in this survey? _____

Tables

This table has many rows and columns. Read it across and down very carefully!

This table shows how many people like different types of vegetables.

Favorite Vegetable		
Type of Vegetable	Number of Votes in 3rd Grade	Number of Votes in 4th Grade
Beans	20	22
Carrots	18	21
Corn	26	26
Peas	35	30

Use the table to answer the questions. Label your answers.

1. How many children in 3rd grade voted for carrots? _____

2. How many children in 4th grade voted for beans? _____

3. How many children in 3rd grade voted for corn? _____

4. Which vegetable do children in 4th grade like best? _____

5. Which vegetable do children in 3rd grade like least? _____

6. Which vegetable got the same number of votes in both grades?_____

7. How many children in 3rd grade voted for beans and corn?

_____

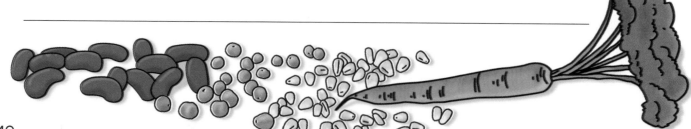

Tally Charts

A **chart** is a way to show a collection of data.

The data in this chart was recorded using **tally marks**. This type of chart is called a tally chart.

This tally chart shows how many people like different types of desserts.

$/ = 1$ $\cancel{||||} = 5$ $\cancel{||||} /// = 8$

Favorite Dessert	
Type of Dessert	Number of Votes
Cake	卌 卌 卌 卌 //
Cookie	卌 卌 卌 卌 卌 卌 ////
Fruit	卌 卌 卌 卌
Ice Cream	卌 卌 卌 卌 卌 //

Use the tally chart to answer the questions. Label your answers.

1. How many children voted for ice cream? _____

2. Show how to count the number of tallies for ice cream.

   _____

3. How many children voted for cake? _____

4. How many children voted for cookies? _____

5. How many children voted for fruit? _____

6. Which dessert is the favorite? _____

7. How many children were in this survey? Count the tallies. _____

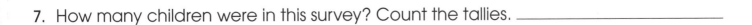

Tally Charts

This tally chart shows how many cups of lemonade were sold at different times of day.

Lemonade Sales	
Time of Day	Cups Sold
10:00 a.m. to 12 p.m.	‖‖‖ ‖‖‖ ‖‖‖ //
12 p.m. to 2:00 p.m.	‖‖‖ ‖‖‖ ‖‖‖ ‖‖‖ ‖‖‖ ‖‖‖ ‖‖‖ ////
2:00 p.m. to 4:00 p.m.	‖‖‖ ‖‖‖ ‖‖‖ ‖‖‖ ‖‖‖ ‖‖‖ ////
4:00 p.m. to 6:00 p.m.	‖‖‖ ‖‖‖ ‖‖‖ ‖‖‖ /

Use the tally chart to answer the questions. Label your answers.

1. How many cups of lemonade were sold from 2:00 p.m. to 4:00 p.m.? _____

2. How many cups of lemonade were sold from 4:00 p.m. to 6:00 p.m.? _____

3. How many cups of lemonade were sold from 12 p.m. to 2:00 p.m.? _____

4. How many cups of lemonade were sold in the morning? _____

5. What is the total number of cups of lemonade sold in the afternoon? _____

6. According to this set of data, when is the best time to have a lemonade stand open? Why?

_____

_____

_____

Tally Charts

1. Complete the tally chart using the data given in the table. Then write the total for each color.

Button Collection	
Color	Number of Buttons
Blue	25
Green	17
Red	32

Button Collection		
Color	Tally	Total
Blue		
Green		
Red		

Use the tally chart to answer the questions. Label your answers.

2. How many green buttons are there? _____

3. How many blue buttons are there? _____

4. There are the most of which color button? _____

5. There are the fewest number of which color button? _____

6. There are more red buttons than green buttons.
   How many more red buttons are there? _____

Make and interpret a tally chart

Tally Charts

1. Complete the tally chart using the data given in the table. Then write the total for each type of hat.

Hat Collection	
Type of Hat	Number of Hats
Baseball Cap	35
Cowboy Hat	16
Stocking Cap	22

Hat Collection		
Type of Hat	Tally	Total
Baseball Cap		
Cowboy Hat		
Stocking Cap		

Use the tally chart to answer the questions. Label your answers.

2. How many stocking caps are there? _____

3. How many cowboy hats are there? _____

4. There are the most of which type of hat? _____

5. Are there more cowboy hats or baseball caps? _____

   How many more are there? _____

6. How many baseball caps, stocking caps, and cowboy hats are there in all?

   _____

Line Plots

A **line plot** can be used to organize and show a collection of data.

The data in this line plot shows the ages of a group of students in a school choir. The number line shows the ages of the students. Each **X** stands for one student.

The **range** is the difference between the greatest and least numbers of the data.

The **mode** is the number that occurs most often.

Members of the School Choir

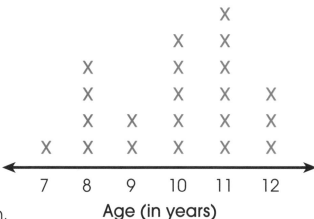

```
                          X
                    X     X
           X        X     X
           X        X  X  X
           X  X  X  X  X  X
        X  X  X  X  X  X
       ◄─────────────────────►
        7  8  9  10 11 12
```

Age (in years)

Use the line plot to answer the questions. Label your answers.

1. How many students are 8 years old? _____

2. How many students are 10 years old? _____

3. How many students are 12 years old? _____

4. What is the mode of this data? _____
   What does the mode tell you?

   _____

5. What is the range of this data? _____
   How did you find it?

   _____

6. How many students are in the choir? _____

7. How many students are younger than 10 years old? _____

Line Plots

The data in this line plot shows the heights of students in a PE class.

Heights of Students in PE Class

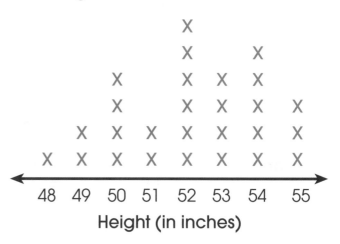

Height (in inches)

Use the line plot to answer the questions. Label your answers.

1. How many students are 50 inches tall? _____

2. How many students are 54 inches tall? _____

3. What is the mode of this data? _____

4. What is the range of this data? _____

5. How many students are 54 inches tall or taller? _____

6. How many students are 50 inches tall or shorter? _____

7. Four students in the class are the same height.
   How tall could they be? List all possible heights. _____

8. How many students are in this class? _____

9. What does this line plot tell you?

_____

Pictographs

A **pictograph** is a way to show a collection of data.

The data in a pictograph can be recorded using pictures or symbols.

This pictograph shows how many students own pets.

Students Who Own Pets	
Type of Pet	Number of Students
Bird	☺ ☺ ☺
Cat	☺ ☺ ☺ ☺ ☺ ☺ ☺ ☺ ☺ ☺ ☺ ☺ ☺ ☺ ☺ ☺
Dog	☺ ☺ ☺ ☺ ☺ ☺ ☺ ☺ ☺ ☺ ☺ ☺ ☺ ☺ ☺ ☺ ☺
Fish	☺ ☺ ☺ ☺ ☺

Each ☺ = 2 students

Use the pictograph to answer the questions. Label your answers.

1. How many students own fish? _____

2. How many students own cats? _____

3. How many students own birds? _____

4. Which type of animal do most students own? _____

   How many students is that? _____

5. How many students own birds and fish? _____

Pictographs

1. Complete the pictograph using the data given in the table.

Make each stand for 5 votes.

Favorite Books	
Type of Book	Number of Votes
Adventure	25
Biography	20
Mystery	10
Science Fiction	15

Favorite Books	
Type of Book	Number of Votes
Adventure	
Biography	
Mystery	
Science Fiction	

Each 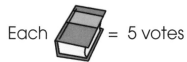 = 5 votes

Use the pictograph to answer the questions. Label your answers.

2. How many symbols did you use for Mystery? _____

   Why? _____

3. How many symbols did you use for Biography? _____

4. Which type of books do students like most? _____

   Do you think this fact is shown better by the table or the pictograph? Explain.

   _____

   _____

Pictographs

Look at this pictograph of students who have collected baseballs autographed by major league players.

As you've learned, the data in a pictograph can be recorded using pictures or symbols.

Sometimes, a pictograph may have half symbols.

Autographed Baseballs	
Name	Number of Baseballs
Sam	⚾ ⚾ ⚾ ⚾ ⚾
Brad	⚾ ⚾ ⚾ ⚾ ⚾ ⚾ ⚾
Emma	⚾ ⚾ ⚾ ⚾ ⚾ ⚾ ◖
Ben	⚾ ⚾ ⚾ ⚾

Each ⚾ = 2 baseballs

If each ⚾ = 2 baseballs, then ◖ = 1 baseball.

Use the pictograph to answer the questions. Label your answers.

1. Who has collected the most autographed baseballs?_____

   How do you know?

   _____

2. How many autographed baseballs does Sam have?_____

3. How many autographed baseballs does Emma have? _____

4. How many autographed baseballs does Ben have?_____

5. How many autographed baseballs do Sam and Emma have?_____

6. Brad has more autographed baseballs than Ben.
   How many more autographed baseballs does Brad have? _____

Pictographs

This pictograph shows how far some students can kick a soccer ball.

Soccer Kicks	
Name	**Distance Kicked**
Anna	⚽ ⚽ ⚽
Roger	⚽ ⚽ ⚽ ⚽ ◖
Beth	⚽ ⚽ ⚽ ⚽
Jose	⚽ ⚽ ⚽ ◖

Each ⚽ = 10 feet

Use the pictograph to answer the questions. Label your answers.

1. If ⚽ = _____ feet, then ◖ = _____ feet.

2. How far can Beth kick a soccer ball? _____

3. How far can Anna kick a soccer ball? _____

4. Who can kick a soccer ball the farthest? _____

   How far is that? _____

5. How much farther can Roger kick a soccer ball than Jose? _____

6. Jack joins the group, and he can kick a soccer ball 55 feet.
   How many symbols will be needed to show this on the pictograph? _____

Bar Graphs

A **graph** is a way to show a collection of data.

The data in this graph uses bars to record data. This type of graph is called a bar graph. Bar graphs may be horizontal or vertical. Read the number at the end of the bar to tell how many.

This bar graph shows how many people own different breeds of dogs.

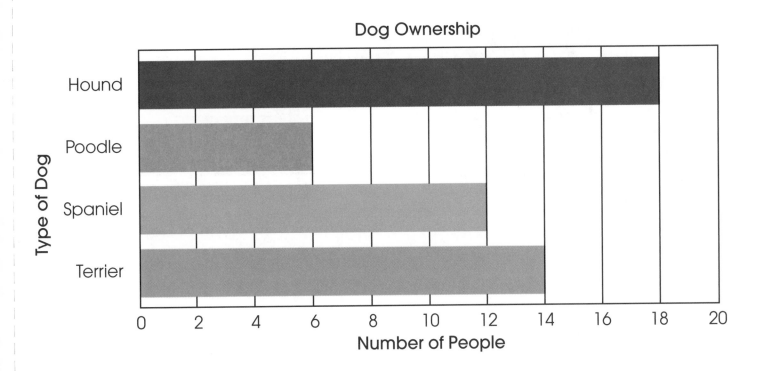

Dog Ownership

Type of Dog: Hound, Poodle, Spaniel, Terrier

Number of People (0 to 20)

Use the graph to answer the questions. Label your answers.

1. How many people own poodles? _____

2. How many people own spaniels? _____

3. How many people own terriers? _____

4. How many people own hounds? _____

5. Which breed of dog is owned by the most people? _____

6. How many people own poodles and terriers? _____

7. More people own hounds than poodles.
   How many more owners have hounds? _____

Bar Graphs

This bar graph shows the weights of some dogs.

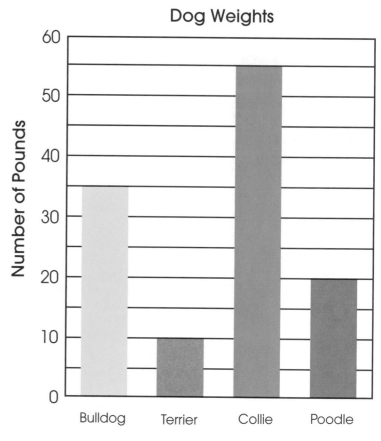

Dog Weights

Type of Dog

Use the graph to answer the questions. Label your answers.

1. How much does the terrier weigh? _____

2. How much does the poodle weigh? _____

3. How much does the bulldog weigh? _____

   How can you tell from the graph? _____

4. How much does the collie weigh? _____

5. List the dogs in order by weight from lightest to heaviest.

   _____ , _____ , _____ , _____

6. How much do the poodle and bulldog weigh in all? _____

7. How much more does the collie weigh than the terrier? _____

Bar Graphs

This bar graph shows how many cats were in a cat show.

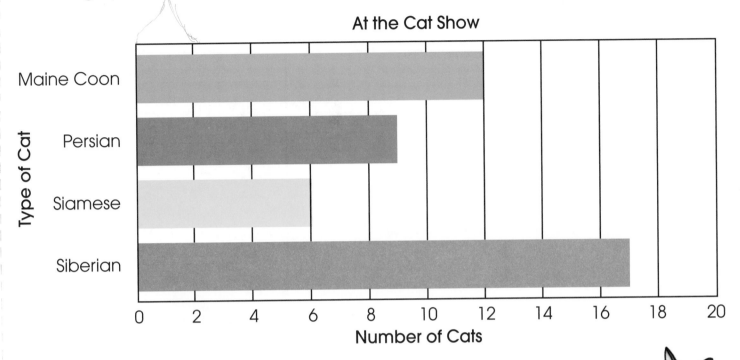

At the Cat Show

Type of Cat

Maine Coon
Persian
Siamese
Siberian

0 2 4 6 8 10 12 14 16 18 20

Number of Cats

Use the graph to answer the questions. Label your answers.

1. How many Siamese cats were in the show? _____

2. How many Persian cats were in the show? _____
   How can you tell from the graph?

   _____

   _____

3. Which breed of cat was there the most of in the show? _____

   How many were there? _____

4. How many Maine Coons were in the show? _____

5. There were more Siberian cats than Siamese cats in the show.

   How many more Siberian cats were there? _____

Bar Graphs

This bar graph shows the number of pets sold at a pet shop in a month.

Use the graph to answer the questions. Label your answers.

1. How many dogs were sold? _____

2. How many birds were sold? _____

3. Which type of pet had the most sales?

   _____

4. How many cats were sold? _____

   How can you tell from the graph?

   _____

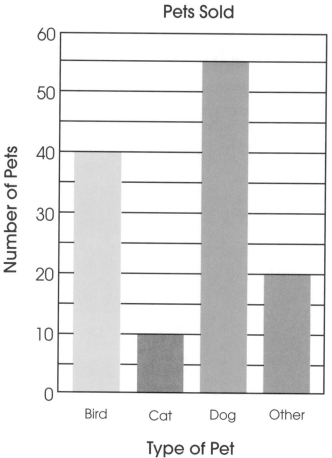

Pets Sold

5. What does the word "Other" mean in the graph? _____

   How many of these pets were sold? _____

6. More dogs were sold than birds.

   How many more dogs were sold? _____

7. How many cats and dogs were sold? _____

8. What was the total number of pets sold during this month?

   _____

Solve word problems using a bar graph

Review Pictographs and Line Plots

This pictograph shows how many cookies some students ate at a picnic.

Write true if the statement is true or false if the statement is not true.

1. Sara ate more cookies than Jenny.

   _____

2. No one ate more cookies than Dave.

   _____

3. Jenny ate 5 cookies.

   _____

4. Mark and Dave ate exactly 7 cookies.

   _____

5. Dave and Jenny ate as many cookies as Mark and Sara.

   _____

Cookies Eaten	
Name	Number of Cookies
Dave	🍪 🍪 🍪 🍪
Jenny	🍪 🍪 🍪
Mark	🍪 🍪 🍪
Sara	🍪 🍪 🍪 🍪

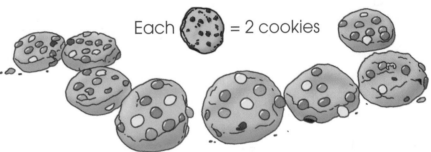

Each 🍪 = 2 cookies

This line plot shows how many students in a certain class have brothers and sisters. Write true if the statement is true or false if the statement is not true.

6. Most students have at least 1 brother or sister.

   _____

7. The mode of this data is 2.

   _____

8. 3 students have no brothers or sisters.

   _____

9. There are 5 students in this class.

   _____

10. 7 students have 3 or more brothers or sisters.

    _____

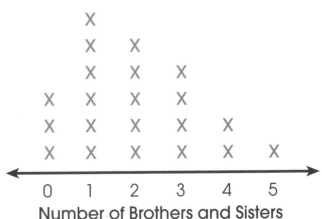

Class Siblings

```
              X
              X   X
              X   X   X
          X   X   X   X
          X   X   X   X   X
          X   X   X   X   X   X
      <----------------------------->
          0   1   2   3   4   5
      Number of Brothers and Sisters
```

Review Tables and Bar Graphs

This table shows the number of students in grades 3 and 4 who are pet owners.

Write true if the statement is true or false if the statement is not true.

1. 21 students in 4th grade own dogs.

   _____

2. More students in each grade own cats than fish.

   _____

3. 20 students in 3rd grade own cats.

   _____

4. There are more fish owners in 4th grade than in 3rd grade.

   _____

5. There are 65 pet owners in 4th grade.

   _____

Students Who Own Pets		
Type of Pet	3rd Grade Students	4th Grade Students
Dog	24	19
Cat	20	21
Bird	8	7
Fish	5	9

This bar graph shows how many students are in after school clubs on each day of the school week.

Write true if the statement is true or false if the statement is not true.

6. 9 students go to after school clubs on Thursday.

   _____

7. More students go to after school clubs on Tuesday than on Thursday.

   _____

8. The most students are in after school clubs on Tuesday.

   _____

9. The most students go to after school clubs in the middle of the week.

   _____

10. More students are in after school clubs on Wednesday than on Monday.

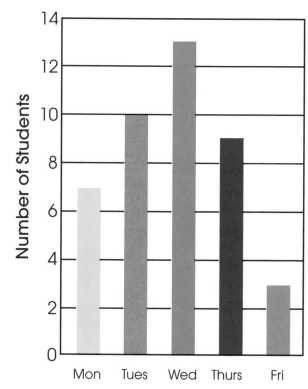

Students in After School Clubs

Bar graph: Number of Students (y-axis, 0 to 14) vs Day of the Week (x-axis)
- Mon: 7
- Tues: 10
- Wed: 13
- Thurs: 9
- Fri: 3

Add or Subtract to Solve Problems

Remember - use these 4 steps to help you solve word problems:

1. **Read** the problem carefully.
2. **Decide** what to do.
3. **Solve** the problem.
4. **Check** to see if the answer makes sense.

Class Fair Tickets Sold		
Day	Children's Tickets	Adult Tickets
Friday	53	15
Saturday	56	22
Sunday	45	40

Use the table to solve the word problems. Show your work. Label your answers.

1. How many class fair tickets were sold on Friday?

2. More adult tickets were sold on Sunday than on Friday. How many more adult tickets were sold on Sunday?

3. What is the total number of children's tickets that were sold?

4. How many adult tickets were sold on Saturday and Sunday?

5. How many class fair tickets were sold in all?

6. Were more tickets sold on Saturday or Sunday? How many more were sold?

Add or Subtract to Solve Problems

Remember:
1. **Read**
2. **Decide**
3. **Solve**
4. **Check**

Students at Area Schools		
School Name	Boys	Girls
Jackson Elementary	378	426
Prairie View Elementary	430	395
Hunter Glen Academy	405	428
Washington Elementary	389	411

Use the table to solve the word problems. Show your work. Label your answers.

1. How many students are at Hunter Glen Academy?

2. There are more boys than girls at Prairie View Elementary. How many more boys are there?

3. About how many students are there at Jackson Elementary School?

4. How many boys are at the elementary schools, not including the academy?

5. How many girls are at Hunter Glen Academy and Prairie View Elementary School?

6. Which school has 800 students?

Thousands, Hundreds, Tens, and Ones

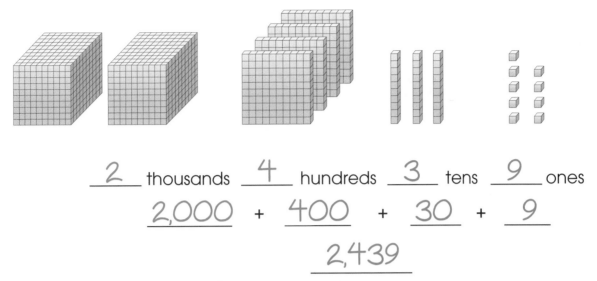

___2___ thousands ___4___ hundreds ___3___ tens ___9___ ones

__2,000__ + __400__ + __30__ + __9__

__2,439__

Look at the picture. Count how many thousands, hundreds, tens, and ones there are. Then write the number.

1.

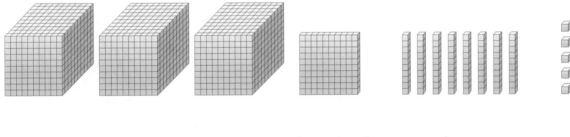

_____ thousands _____ hundred _____ tens _____ ones

_____ + _____ + _____ + _____

_____

2.

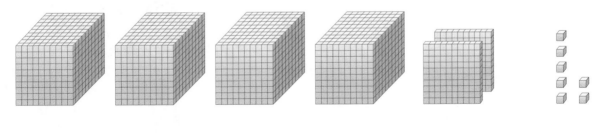

_____ thousands _____ hundreds _____ tens _____ ones

_____ + _____ + _____ + _____

_____

Place Value of Four-Digit Numbers

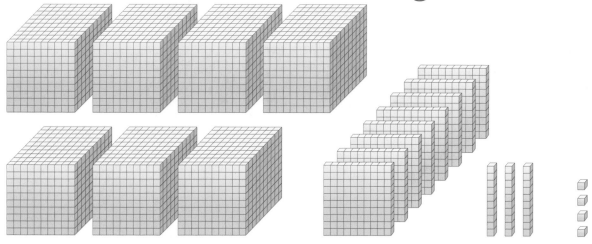

7,834 = **7** thousands **8** hundreds **3** tens **4** ones

In the number, one digit is in boldface type.
Circle the place value of that digit.

1. 2,43**5**   thousands   hundreds   tens   (ones)

2. 8,**2**59   thousands   hundreds   tens   ones

3. **1**,020   thousands   hundreds   tens   ones

4. **2**,435   thousands   hundreds   tens   ones

5. 9,5**4**1   thousands   hundreds   tens   ones

6. 1,02**0**   thousands   hundreds   tens   ones

Circle the correct digit in the number.

7. Circle the ones.   8 , 1 9 (1)

8. Circle the thousands.   4 , 2 7 5

9. Circle the hundreds.   1 , 2 4 3

10. Circle the tens.   9 , 4 7 0

11. Circle the thousands.   5 , 4 3 7

12. Circle the hundreds.   9 , 7 5 1

Understanding Greater Numbers

Find the sum or number to fill in the puzzle.

Across

1. 2 hundreds + 6 tens + 8 ones
3. 3 hundreds + 9 tens + 7 ones
5. 4 thousands + 7 hundreds + 8 tens + 0 ones
7. three thousand three hundred thirty-three
8. 9,000 + 30 + 5
9. six hundred twenty-two
11. 6 hundreds + 7 tens + 8 ones
13. 5,000 + 300 + 90
15. 8 thousands + 1 hundred + 2 tens + 6 ones
16. 90 + 100
17. two thousand five hundred fifty

Down

1. 2 thousands + 9 hundreds + 5 tens + 9 ones
2. eight thousand four hundred thirty-three
3. 3,000 + 30 + 6
4. 7 thousands + 3 hundreds + 9 tens + 2 ones
6. 4 + 50 + 300 + 7,000
10. two thousand five hundred ninety-nine
11. 600 + 80 + 5
12. 20 + 2 + 800
14. 3 hundreds + 1 ten

Puzzle grid:

1. 2	6	2. 8		3.		4.
9		5.	6.			
5		7.				
8. 9				9.	10.	
11.		12.	13.	14.		
15.				16.		
		17.				

Greater or Less

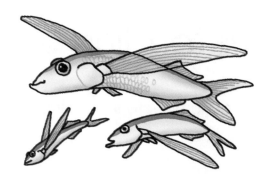

1,525 is **greater** than 1,520.
    1,52<u>5</u> > 1,52<u>0</u>.

Which digits did you compare? _____ones_____

2,650 is **less** than 3,210.
    <u>2</u>,650 < <u>3</u>,210

Which digits did you compare? _thousands_

Compare the numbers. Then write < or > in the ◯.

1. 5,148 ◯ 4,185   Which digits did you compare?   _____
2. 6,450 ◯ 6,504   Which digits did you compare?   _____
3. 5,709 ◯ 5,704   Which digits did you compare?   _____
4. 9,205 ◯ 9,250   Which digits did you compare?   _____
5. 3,239 ◯ 3,299   Which digits did you compare?   _____
6. 4,398 ◯ 2,459   Which digits did you compare?   _____
7. 2,879 ◯ 2,814   Which digits did you compare?   _____

Write the numbers in order from **least** to **greatest**.

8. 6,705, 6,075, 6,507,   675   _____, _____, _____, _____

9. 4,279, 7,942,   987, 4,297   _____, _____, _____, _____

10. 6,502,   506, 6,052,   56   _____, _____, _____, _____

Challenge: Write the **greatest** four-digit
           number you can using the digits
           3, 9, 1, and 6.   _____

Super Challenge: On another sheet of paper, write as many four-digit numbers
                as you can using the digits 3, 9, 1, and 6. Then put all the
                numbers in order.

Round Four-Digit Numbers

To **round** a number to the **nearest thousand**, look at the **hundreds** place.
If the digit in the hundreds place is **5 or more**, then **round up**.
If the digit in the hundreds place is **4 or less**, then **round down**.

Is 3,760 closer to 3,000 or 4,000?

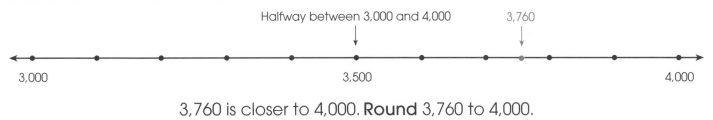

Halfway between 3,000 and 4,000   3,760

3,000   3,500   4,000

3,760 is closer to 4,000. **Round** 3,760 to 4,000.

The hundreds digit is more than 5.

Look at the boldface number. To round, circle the nearest thousand.

1. **2,833**   2,000   3,000   2. **7,250**   7,000   8,000   3. **4,050**   4,000   5,000

4. **2,083**   2,000   3,000   5. **7,500**   7,000   8,000   6. **4,550**   4,000   5,000

7. **2,480**   2,000   3,000   8. **7,590**   7,000   8,000   9. **4,005**   4,000   5,000

Round the number to the nearest thousand.

10. 3,470 _____   11. 6,090 _____   12. 5,150 _____

13. 3,047 _____   14. 6,450 _____   15. 8,500 _____

16. 3,740 _____   17. 6,509 _____   18. 7,059 _____

Round the number to the nearest hundred.

19. 1,579 _1,600_   20. 4,743 _____

21. 2,746 _____   22. 3,729 _____

23. 6,555 _____   24. 5,555 _____

> Do you remember how to round numbers to the nearest hundred? Look at the tens digit.

Estimate Sums and Differences

Estimate sums and differences by **rounding** to the **nearest thousand**.

Estimate the sum.

Estimate:
```
  5,279  →    5,000
+ 3,540  →  + 4,000
             9,000
```

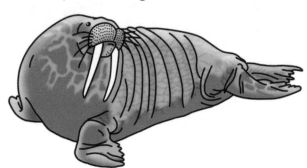

Estimate the difference.

Estimate:
```
  7,318  →    7,000
- 3,645  →  - 4,000
             3,000
```

Round the numbers to the nearest thousand.
Write the estimate for the sum or difference.

1.

Estimate:

```
  6,371  →  _____

+ 4,238  →  + _____
```

2.

Estimate:

```
  7,500  →  _____

- 1,095  →  - _____
```

3.

Estimate:

```
  3,475  →  _____

- 1,847  →  - _____
```

4.

Estimate:

```
  2,535  →  _____

+ 2,359  →  + _____
```

Estimate the sum or difference.

5. 2,846 + 3,081 _____

6. 8,155 - 2,099 _____

7. 4,666 - 3,008 _____

8. 3,463 + 2,905 _____

9. 8,509 + 750 _____

10. 5,863 - 608 _____

Add Four-Digit Numbers

Add the **ones**.
Regroup as needed.

$$
\begin{array}{r}
7,2\overset{1}{8}6 \\
+\ 2,465 \\
\hline
1
\end{array}
$$

Add the **tens**.
Regroup as needed.

$$
\begin{array}{r}
7,\overset{1}{2}\overset{1}{8}6 \\
+\ 2,465 \\
\hline
51
\end{array}
$$

Add the **hundreds**.
Regroup as needed.

$$
\begin{array}{r}
7,\overset{1}{2}\overset{1}{8}6 \\
+\ 2,465 \\
\hline
751
\end{array}
$$

Add the **thousands**.

$$
\begin{array}{r}
\overset{1}{7},\overset{1}{2}86 \\
+\ 2,465 \\
\hline
9,751
\end{array}
$$

Write the sum.

1.
$$
\begin{array}{r}
4,840 \\
+\ 1,023 \\
\hline
\end{array}
$$

2.
$$
\begin{array}{r}
4,462 \\
+\ 1,923 \\
\hline
\end{array}
$$

3.
$$
\begin{array}{r}
2,640 \\
+\ 3,173 \\
\hline
\end{array}
$$

4.
$$
\begin{array}{r}
6,540 \\
+\ 2,482 \\
\hline
\end{array}
$$

5.
$$
\begin{array}{r}
7,731 \\
+\ 1,273 \\
\hline
\end{array}
$$

6.
$$
\begin{array}{r}
1,847 \\
+\ 6,259 \\
\hline
\end{array}
$$

7.
$$
\begin{array}{r}
4,787 \\
+\ 1,896 \\
\hline
\end{array}
$$

8.
$$
\begin{array}{r}
6,354 \\
+\ 2,498 \\
\hline
\end{array}
$$

9.
$$
\begin{array}{r}
2,743 \\
+\ 5,189 \\
\hline
\end{array}
$$

10.
$$
\begin{array}{r}
3,086 \\
+\ 5,027 \\
\hline
\end{array}
$$

11.
$$
\begin{array}{r}
6,259 \\
+\ 1,362 \\
\hline
\end{array}
$$

12.
$$
\begin{array}{r}
4,274 \\
+\ 3,899 \\
\hline
\end{array}
$$

Subtract Four-Digit Numbers

Subtract the **ones**. Regroup as needed.	Subtract the **tens**. Regroup as needed.	Subtract the **hundreds**. Regroup as needed.	Subtract the **thousands**.	Check:

$$\begin{array}{r} 2,63\boxed{7} \\ -\ 1,71\boxed{5} \\ \hline \boxed{2} \end{array}$$

7 − 5 = 2
No regrouping.

$$\begin{array}{r} 2,6\boxed{3}7 \\ -\ 1,7\boxed{1}5 \\ \hline \boxed{2}2 \end{array}$$

3 − 1 = 2
No regrouping.

$$\begin{array}{r} \overset{1}{2},\overset{16}{\cancel{6}}37 \\ -\ 1,\boxed{7}15 \\ \hline \boxed{9}22 \end{array}$$

6 − 7 = ?
Regroup.

$$\begin{array}{r} \overset{1}{\cancel{2}},\overset{16}{\cancel{6}}37 \\ -\ \boxed{1},715 \\ \hline 922 \end{array}$$

1 − 1 = 0, but do not write a 0 as the first digit of a number.
The **difference** is **922**.

$$\begin{array}{r} \overset{1}{}\ 922 \\ +\ 1,715 \\ \hline 2,637 \end{array}$$

Write the difference.

1. $\begin{array}{r} 4,345 \\ -\ 3,261 \\ \hline \end{array}$

2. $\begin{array}{r} 5,916 \\ -\ 2,842 \\ \hline \end{array}$

3. $\begin{array}{r} 2,135 \\ -\ 1,841 \\ \hline \end{array}$

4. $\begin{array}{r} 8,642 \\ -\ 7,539 \\ \hline \end{array}$

5. $\begin{array}{r} 6,757 \\ -\ 4,902 \\ \hline \end{array}$

6. $\begin{array}{r} 3,502 \\ -\ 1,201 \\ \hline \end{array}$

7. $\begin{array}{r} 8,435 \\ -\ 5,713 \\ \hline \end{array}$

8. $\begin{array}{r} 6,149 \\ -\ 2,076 \\ \hline \end{array}$

9. $\begin{array}{r} 5,806 \\ -\ 3,402 \\ \hline \end{array}$

10. $\begin{array}{r} 4,490 \\ -\ 1,374 \\ \hline \end{array}$

11. $\begin{array}{r} 7,261 \\ -\ 3,521 \\ \hline \end{array}$

12. $\begin{array}{r} 9,214 \\ -\ 7,007 \\ \hline \end{array}$

Subtract Four-Digit Numbers

Subtract the **ones**. Regroup as needed.	Subtract the **tens**. Regroup as needed.	Subtract the **hundreds**. Regroup as needed.	Subtract the **thousands**.	Check:
$\overset{4}{\cancel{5}},\overset{9}{\cancel{0}}\overset{9}{\cancel{0}}\overset{14}{\cancel{4}}$ $-\ 1,4\ 9\ 6$ $\underline{\qquad 8}$	$\overset{4}{\cancel{5}},\overset{9}{\cancel{0}}\overset{9}{\cancel{0}}\overset{14}{\cancel{4}}$ $-\ 1,4\ 9\ 6$ $\underline{\qquad 0\ 8}$	$\overset{4}{\cancel{5}},\overset{9}{\cancel{0}}\overset{9}{\cancel{0}}\overset{14}{\cancel{4}}$ $-\ 1,4\ 9\ 6$ $\underline{\qquad 5\ 0\ 8}$	$\overset{4}{\cancel{5}},\overset{9}{\cancel{0}}\overset{9}{\cancel{0}}\overset{14}{\cancel{4}}$ $-\ 1,4\ 9\ 6$ $\underline{3,5\ 0\ 8}$	$\overset{1}{\ }\overset{1}{\ }\overset{1}{\ }$ $3,5\ 0\ 8$ $+1,4\ 9\ 6$ $\underline{5,0\ 0\ 4}$

$4 - 6 = ?$
Regroup. You cannot regroup 0 tens. Since 5,000 is the same as 500 tens, regroup 500 tens to 499 tens and 1 ten.
$14 - 6 = 8$

$9 - 9 = 0$

$9 - 4 = 5$

$4 - 1 = 3$
The **difference** is **3,508**.

Write the difference.

1. 3,005
    − 1,527

2. 7,002
    − 3,595

3. 6,000
    − 4,136

4. 5,500
    − 1,275

5. 4,003
    − 1,249

6. 2,008
    − 1,509

7. 8,050
    − 4,999

8. 9,000
    − 3,472

9. 8,070
    − 1,358

10. 7,003
    − 2,469

11. 3,001
    − 2,894

12. 9,400
    − 3,406

13. 9,005
    − 4,039

14. 8,067
    − 1,663

15. 6,003
    − 2,086

16. 3,003
    − 1,008

Find Sums and Differences

Find the sums and differences to fill in the puzzle.

Across

1. 346 + 62 = _____

3. 873 – 189 = _____

5. 103 – 85 = _____

6. 198 + 6 = _____

7. 435 + 168 + 53 = _____

9. 593 – 199 = _____

11. 66 + 6 = _____

12. 5,540 – 1,234 = _____

13. 99 + 9 + 90 = _____

Down

1. 29 + 291 + 92 = _____

2. 643 + 7,500 = _____

4. 2,053 – 1,168 = _____

7. 4,567 + 1,865 = _____

8. 864 – 258 = _____

10. 732 – 638 = _____

11. 46 + 6 + 19 = _____

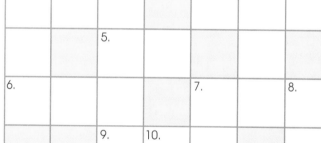

Practice adding and subtracting

Add or Subtract to Solve Problems

Remember:
1. **Read**
2. **Decide**
3. **Solve**
4. **Check**

Solve the problems. Show your work. Label your answers.

1. The class is working on a 1,500-piece jigsaw puzzle. There are 793 unused pieces left. How many pieces have already been used in the puzzle?

2. The U.S.-Mexican border is 1,933 miles long. The U.S.-Canadian border is 3,987 miles long. Which border is longer? How much longer is it?

3. The Willis Tower in Chicago is 1,450 feet tall. The Empire State Building in New York is 1,250 feet tall. Which building is taller? How much taller is it?

4. Jeff's grandfather was born in 1949. How old was Jeff's grandfather in 2007?

5. Use the digits 1 through 8 only once each to create the greatest four-digit number possible and the least four-digit number possible. What is the sum of these two numbers?

6. Use the digits 1 through 8 only once each to create the greatest four-digit number possible and the least four-digit number possible. What is the difference between these two numbers?

Add or Subtract to Solve Problems

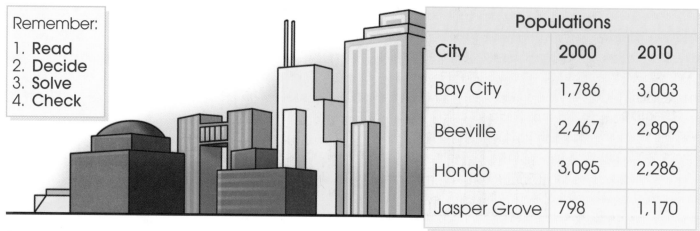

Remember:
1. **Read**
2. **Decide**
3. **Solve**
4. **Check**

Populations		
City	2000	2010
Bay City	1,786	3,003
Beeville	2,467	2,809
Hondo	3,095	2,286
Jasper Grove	798	1,170

Solve the problems. Show your work. Label your answers.

1. How many more people did Bay City have in 2010 than in 2000?

2. What is the total population for all four cities in 2000?

3. How many more people lived in Hondo than in Beeville in 2000?

4. About how many people were there in all four cities in 2010?

5. What is the difference in population between the largest city and the smallest city in 2010?

6. Which city had a smaller population in 2010 than in 2000? How many fewer people were there?

Introduction to Multiplication

There are **3** groups of bats.
There are **2** bats in each group.

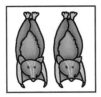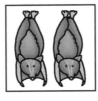

$$3 \times 2 = 6$$

factor factor product

The answer to a multiplication problem is called the **product**.

Look at the picture. Write the missing factor.
Then write the product.

1.

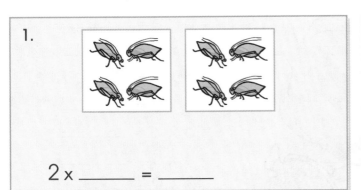

$2 \times \underline{\hspace{1cm}} = \underline{\hspace{1cm}}$

2.

$2 \times \underline{\hspace{1cm}} = \underline{\hspace{1cm}}$

3.

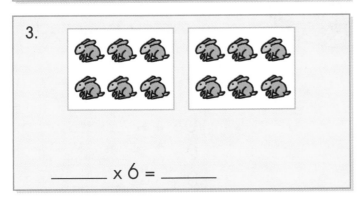

$\underline{\hspace{1cm}} \times 6 = \underline{\hspace{1cm}}$

4.

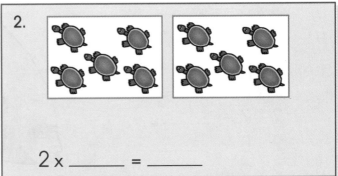

$3 \times \underline{\hspace{1cm}} = \underline{\hspace{1cm}}$

5.

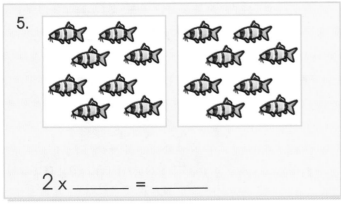

$2 \times \underline{\hspace{1cm}} = \underline{\hspace{1cm}}$

6.

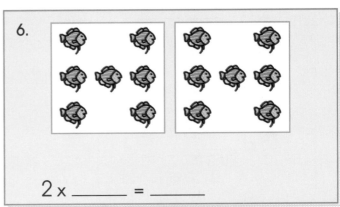

$2 \times \underline{\hspace{1cm}} = \underline{\hspace{1cm}}$

Multiply by 0, 1, 2, and 3

You can also think of multiplication as **repeated addition**.

5 + 5 + 5 = 15

3 x 5 = _15_

Write the products.

1.

Multiply by 2
2 x 1 = _____
2 x 2 = _____
2 x 3 = _____
2 x 4 = _____
2 x 5 = _____
2 x 6 = _____
2 x 7 = _____
2 x 8 = _____
2 x 9 = _____

Count by **2s** to check your answers.

2.

Multiply by 3
3 x 1 = _____
3 x 2 = _____
3 x 3 = _____
3 x 4 = _____
3 x 5 = _____
3 x 6 = _____
3 x 7 = _____
3 x 8 = _____
3 x 9 = _____

Count by **3s** to check your answers.

3.

Multiply by 1
1 x 1 = _____
1 x 2 = _____
1 x 3 = _____
1 x 4 = _____
1 x 5 = _____
1 x 6 = _____
1 x 7 = _____
1 x 8 = _____
1 x 9 = _____

Hint: Any number times **1** equals that number.

4.

Multiply by 0
0 x 1 = _____
0 x 2 = _____
0 x 3 = _____
0 x 4 = _____
0 x 5 = _____
0 x 6 = _____
0 x 7 = _____
0 x 8 = _____
0 x 9 = _____

Hint: Any number times **0** equals **0**.

Multiply by 4 and 5

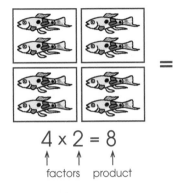 =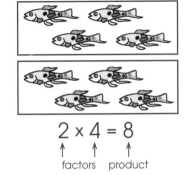

$4 \times 2 = 8$

↑ ↑ ↑
factors product

$2 \times 4 = 8$

↑ ↑ ↑
factors product

Commutative Property of Multiplication

Changing the **order** of the factors does not change the product.

$4 \times 2 = 2 \times 4$

$8 = 8$

Write the products.

1.

Multiply by 4
$4 \times 1 =$ _____
$4 \times 2 =$ _____
$4 \times 3 =$ _____
$4 \times 4 =$ _____
$4 \times 5 =$ _____
$4 \times 6 =$ _____
$4 \times 7 =$ _____
$4 \times 8 =$ _____
$4 \times 9 =$ _____

Count by **4s** to check your answers.

2.

Multiply by 5
$5 \times 1 =$ _____
$5 \times 2 =$ _____
$5 \times 3 =$ _____
$5 \times 4 =$ _____
$5 \times 5 =$ _____
$5 \times 6 =$ _____
$5 \times 7 =$ _____
$5 \times 8 =$ _____
$5 \times 9 =$ _____

Count by **5s** to check your answers.

Practice these facts.

3. $4 \times 5 =$ _____
4. $0 \times 8 =$ _____
5. $3 \times 3 =$ _____
6. $5 \times 4 =$ _____
7. $5 \times 7 =$ _____
8. $3 \times 7 =$ _____
9. $5 \times 1 =$ _____
10. $4 \times 8 =$ _____
11. $3 \times 6 =$ _____
12. $5 \times 9 =$ _____
13. $2 \times 7 =$ _____
14. $2 \times 5 =$ _____
15. $4 \times 3 =$ _____
16. $4 \times 4 =$ _____
17. $2 \times 9 =$ _____
18. $4 \times 7 =$ _____

Practice Multiplication Facts

Find the products.

Multiply by 6 and 7

$4 + 4 + 4 + 4 + 4 + 4 + 4 = \underline{28}$

$7 \times 4 = \underline{28}$

Write the products.

1.
Multiply by 6
$6 \times 1 = \underline{\hspace{1.5cm}}$
$6 \times 2 = \underline{\hspace{1.5cm}}$
$6 \times 3 = \underline{\hspace{1.5cm}}$
$6 \times 4 = \underline{\hspace{1.5cm}}$
$6 \times 5 = \underline{\hspace{1.5cm}}$
$6 \times 6 = \underline{\hspace{1.5cm}}$
$6 \times 7 = \underline{\hspace{1.5cm}}$
$6 \times 8 = \underline{\hspace{1.5cm}}$
$6 \times 9 = \underline{\hspace{1.5cm}}$

Count by **6s** to check your answers.

2.
Multiply by 7
$7 \times 1 = \underline{\hspace{1.5cm}}$
$7 \times 2 = \underline{\hspace{1.5cm}}$
$7 \times 3 = \underline{\hspace{1.5cm}}$
$7 \times 4 = \underline{\hspace{1.5cm}}$
$7 \times 5 = \underline{\hspace{1.5cm}}$
$7 \times 6 = \underline{\hspace{1.5cm}}$
$7 \times 7 = \underline{\hspace{1.5cm}}$
$7 \times 8 = \underline{\hspace{1.5cm}}$
$7 \times 9 = \underline{\hspace{1.5cm}}$

Count by **7s** to check your answers.

Write the missing factor or product.

3. $5 \times \underline{\hspace{1.5cm}} = 15$

4. $6 \times \underline{\hspace{1.5cm}} = 0$

5. $\underline{\hspace{1.5cm}} \times 7 = 14$

6. $4 \times 6 = \underline{\hspace{1.5cm}}$

7. $3 \times 9 = \underline{\hspace{1.5cm}}$

8. $7 \times \underline{\hspace{1.5cm}} = 56$

9. $2 \times \underline{\hspace{1.5cm}} = 18$

10. $\underline{\hspace{1.5cm}} \times 5 = 35$

11. $4 \times \underline{\hspace{1.5cm}} = 24$

12. $\underline{\hspace{1.5cm}} \times 5 = 30$

13. $7 \times \underline{\hspace{1.5cm}} = 7$

14. $\underline{\hspace{1.5cm}} \times 9 = 54$

Triangle Times

Write a product in each circle.

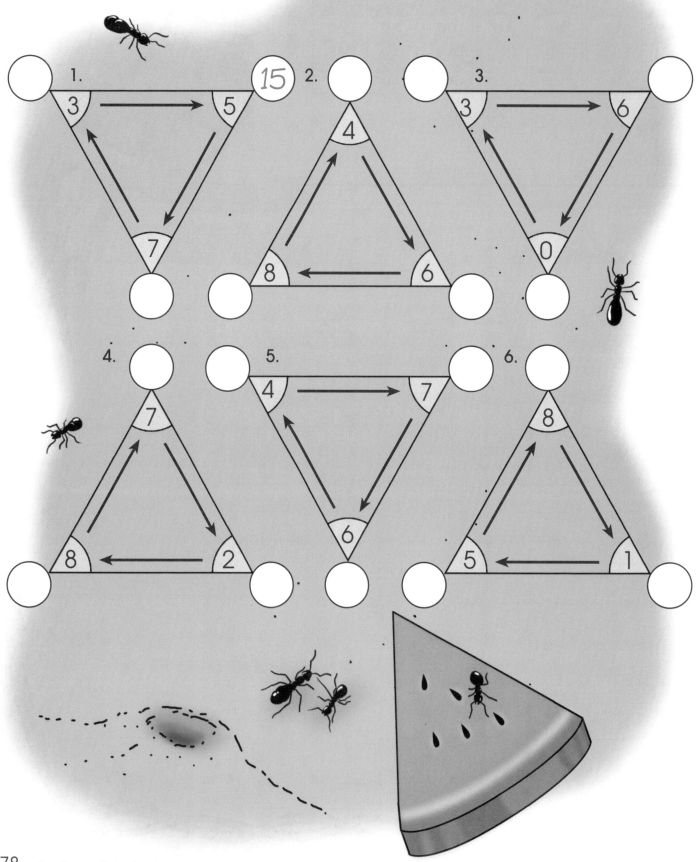

Multiply by 8 and 9

Write the products.

1.

Multiply by 8
8 x 1 = _____
8 x 2 = _____
8 x 3 = _____
8 x 4 = _____
8 x 5 = _____
8 x 6 = _____
8 x 7 = _____
8 x 8 = _____
8 x 9 = _____

Count by **8s** to check your answers.

2.

Multiply by 9	Find the sum of the product's digits:
9 x 1 = _____	0 + 9 = ___9___
9 x 2 = _____	1 + 8 = ___9___
9 x 3 = _____	2 + 7 = _____
9 x 4 = _____	3 + 6 = _____
9 x 5 = _____	4 + _____ = _____
9 x 6 = _____	5 + _____ = _____
9 x 7 = _____	_____ + 3 = _____
9 x 8 = _____	_____ + 2 = _____
9 x 9 = _____	8 + _____ = _____

When 9 is multiplied by a single digit, the digits of the product always have a sum of 9.

3. Fill in the multiplication table. Write the products.

x	0	1	2	3	4	5	6	7	8	9
0	0				0					
1		1					6			
2										
3										
4		4								
5										
6							36			
7	0									
8										
9										

Factor Turn-Arounds

Remember the **Commutative Property of Multiplication-**
Changing the order of the factors does not change the product.

If you know 5 x 3, then you know 3 x 5.
5 x 3 = 15 and 3 x 5 = 15

Write the missing factor or product.

1. 4 x 2 = _____

    2 x 4 = _____

2. 3 x 7 = _____

    7 x 3 = _____

3. 5 x 9 = _____

    9 x 5 = _____

4. 6 x 8 = _____

    8 x 6 = _____

5. 9 x 4 = _____

    4 x 9 = _____

6. 7 x _____ = 63

    9 x 7 = _____

7. 5 x 8 = _____

    8 x _____ = 40

8. 7 x 6 = _____

    6 x _____ = 42

9. _____ x 9 = 27

    9 x 3 = _____

10. 9 x 6 = _____

    6 x _____ = 54

11. 7 x _____ = 0

    _____ x 7 = 0

12. 8 x _____ = 8

    1 x 8 = _____

Write the product and the related multiplication fact.

13. If I know that 6 x 5 = _____ , then I also know that __5__ x _____ = _____ .

14. If I know that 9 x 7 = _____ , then I also know that _____ x _____ = _____ .

15. If I know that 8 x 9 = _____ , then I also know that _____ x _____ = _____ .

16. If I know that 9 x 6 = _____ , then I also know that _____ x _____ = _____ .

Practice multiplication facts; commutative property

Practice Multiplication Facts

Find the products to fill in the puzzle.

Across

1. 5
   × 2

2. 8
   × 3

3. 5
   × 6

4. 4
   × 3

5. 8
   × 2

6. 7
   × 5

7. 6
   × 2

8. 2
   × 9

9. 8
   × 5

10. 5
    × 5

11. 3
    × 7

12. 8
    × 3

Down

1. 7
   × 2

2. 5
   × 4

3. 8
   × 4

4. 4
   × 4

5. 5
   × 3

6. 4
   × 8

7. 6
   × 3

8. 2
   × 5

9. 9
   × 5

10. 7
    × 3

11. 4
    × 6

12. 7
    × 4

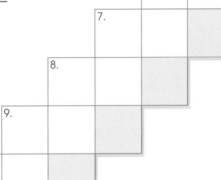

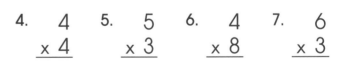

Fast Facts!

Time yourself. Can you do all of these problems in less than 10 minutes?

1. $3 \times 6 =$ _____	13. $7 \times 1 =$ _____	25. $4 \times 6 =$ _____	37. $0 \times 3 =$ _____
2. $5 \times 5 =$ _____	14. $4 \times 3 =$ _____	26. $2 \times 9 =$ _____	38. $7 \times 8 =$ _____
3. $8 \times 3 =$ _____	15. $6 \times 6 =$ _____	27. $5 \times 9 =$ _____	39. $4 \times 7 =$ _____
4. $9 \times 9 =$ _____	16. $5 \times 8 =$ _____	28. $7 \times 7 =$ _____	40. $6 \times 2 =$ _____
5. $3 \times 7 =$ _____	17. $9 \times 6 =$ _____	29. $8 \times 4 =$ _____	41. $7 \times 9 =$ _____
6. $0 \times 8 =$ _____	18. $3 \times 9 =$ _____	30. $8 \times 8 =$ _____	42. $6 \times 5 =$ _____
7. $9 \times 5 =$ _____	19. $4 \times 7 =$ _____	31. $4 \times 2 =$ _____	43. $9 \times 1 =$ _____
8. $6 \times 8 =$ _____	20. $8 \times 9 =$ _____	32. $7 \times 0 =$ _____	44. $4 \times 4 =$ _____
9. $6 \times 4 =$ _____	21. $9 \times 7 =$ _____	33. $8 \times 6 =$ _____	45. $9 \times 4 =$ _____
10. $8 \times 7 =$ _____	22. $2 \times 9 =$ _____	34. $7 \times 6 =$ _____	46. $6 \times 9 =$ _____
11. $4 \times 9 =$ _____	23. $6 \times 7 =$ _____	35. $9 \times 8 =$ _____	47. $7 \times 3 =$ _____
12. $5 \times 7 =$ _____	24. $4 \times 8 =$ _____	36. $3 \times 3 =$ _____	48. $8 \times 5 =$ _____

Introduction to Division

You can use division to find the number in each group or the number of groups.

Find the number in each group:

There are 8 in all.
Divide the 8 into 2 groups.
How many are in each group? __4__

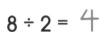

$8 \div 2 =$ __4__

Find the number of groups:

There are 8 in all.
There are 4 in each group.
How many groups of 4
are there? __2__

$8 \div 4 =$ __2__

Read the problem. Circle the correct number of groups.
Answer the question and fill in the blanks.

1.

There are 12 in all.
There are 4 in each group.
How many groups of 4 are there? _____

$12 \div 4 =$ _____

2.

There are 15 in all.
Divide the 15 into 3 groups.
How many are in each group? _____

$15 \div 3 =$ _____

3.

There are _____ in all.
Divide the _____ into 2 groups.
How many are in each group? _____

_____ $\div$ 2 = _____

4.

There are _____ in all.
Divide the _____ into 4 groups.
How many are in each group? _____

_____ $\div$ 4 = _____

5.

There are _____ in all.
There are 3 in each group.
How many groups of 3 are there? _____

_____ $\div$ 3 = _____

6.

There are _____ in all.
There are 6 in each group.
How many groups of 6 are there? _____

_____ $\div$ _____ = _____

Divide by 2

How many groups of **2** are in **16**? _8_

$16 \div 2 = 8$

↑ dividend ↑ divisor ↑ quotient

Look at the picture. Circle groups of 2.
Answer the question. Write the quotient.

1.

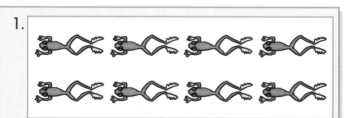

How many groups of 2 are in 8?_____

$8 \div 2 =$ _____

2.

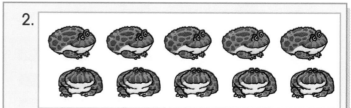

How many groups of 2 are in 10?_____

$10 \div 2 =$ _____

3.

How many groups of 2 are in 14? _____

$14 \div 2 =$ _____

4.

How many groups of 2 are in 12? _____

$12 \div 2 =$ _____

Write the quotients.

5.

Divide by 2	
$2 \div 2 =$ _____	$12 \div 2 =$ _____
$4 \div 2 =$ _____	$14 \div 2 =$ _____
$6 \div 2 =$ _____	$16 \div 2 =$ _____
$8 \div 2 =$ _____	$18 \div 2 =$ _____
$10 \div 2 =$ _____	

Divide by 3

How many groups of **3** are in **24**? _8_

24 ÷ 3 = _8_

Look at the picture. Circle groups of 3.
Answer the question. Write the quotient.

1.

How many groups of 3 are in 12? _____

12 ÷ 3 = ____

2.

How many groups of 3 are in 15? _____

15 ÷ 3 = ____

3.

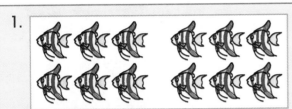

How many groups of 3 are in 18? _____

18 ÷ 3 = ____

4.

How many groups of 3 are in 21? _____

21 ÷ 3 = ____

Write the quotients.

5.

Divide by 3	
3 ÷ 3 = _____	18 ÷ 3 = _____
6 ÷ 3 = _____	21 ÷ 3 = _____
9 ÷ 3 = _____	24 ÷ 3 = _____
12 ÷ 3 = _____	27 ÷ 3 = _____
15 ÷ 3 = _____	

Divide by 4 and 5

How many groups of **5** are in **15**? ___3___

$15 \div 5 =$ ___3___

Write the quotients.

1.

Divide by 4
$4 \div 4 =$ _____
$8 \div 4 =$ _____
$12 \div 4 =$ _____
$16 \div 4 =$ _____
$20 \div 4 =$ _____
$24 \div 4 =$ _____
$28 \div 4 =$ _____
$32 \div 4 =$ _____
$36 \div 4 =$ _____

2.

Divide by 5
$5 \div 5 =$ _____
$10 \div 5 =$ _____
$15 \div 5 =$ _____
$20 \div 5 =$ _____
$25 \div 5 =$ _____
$30 \div 5 =$ _____
$35 \div 5 =$ _____
$40 \div 5 =$ _____
$45 \div 5 =$ _____

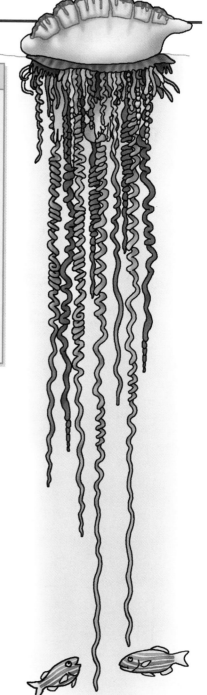

Write the quotient.

3. $6 \div 3 =$ _____
5. $10 \div 2 =$ _____
7. $20 \div 4 =$ _____
9. $20 \div 5 =$ _____
11. $25 \div 5 =$ _____
13. $8 \div 4 =$ _____
15. $16 \div 4 =$ _____
17. $21 \div 3 =$ _____

4. $4 \div 2 =$ _____
6. $15 \div 5 =$ _____
8. $14 \div 2 =$ _____
10. $12 \div 3 =$ _____
12. $18 \div 2 =$ _____
14. $10 \div 5 =$ _____
16. $12 \div 2 =$ _____
18. $28 \div 4 =$ _____

Divide by 6 and 7

Knowing multiplication facts can
help you recall division facts.

Here is a multiplication fact: $6 \times 3 = 18$

Here are two related division facts: $18 \div 3 = 6$
$18 \div 6 = 3$

Write the quotients. Recall related multiplication facts if you need help.

1.

Divide by 6
$6 \div 6 =$ _____
$12 \div 6 =$ _____
$18 \div 6 =$ _____
$24 \div 6 =$ _____
$30 \div 6 =$ _____
$36 \div 6 =$ _____
$42 \div 6 =$ _____
$48 \div 6 =$ _____
$54 \div 6 =$ _____

2.

Divide by 7
$7 \div 7 =$ _____
$14 \div 7 =$ _____
$21 \div 7 =$ _____
$28 \div 7 =$ _____
$35 \div 7 =$ _____
$42 \div 7 =$ _____
$49 \div 7 =$ _____
$56 \div 7 =$ _____
$63 \div 7 =$ _____

Write the missing dividend, divisor, or quotient.

3. $12 \div$ _____ $= 2$

4. $56 \div$ _____ $= 8$

5. $35 \div$ _____ $= 5$

6. $54 \div 6 =$ _____

7. _____ $\div 6 = 5$

8. _____ $\div 6 = 7$

9. $49 \div 7 =$ _____

10. $7 \div$ _____ $= 1$

11. $48 \div$ _____ $= 8$

12. $36 \div$ _____ $= 6$

Divide by 6 and 7; multiplication and division facts relationship

Divide by 8 and 9

Think of related multiplication facts to find the quotients.

Write the quotients. Recall related multiplication facts if you need help.

1.

Divide by 8
8 ÷ 8 = _____
16 ÷ 8 = _____
24 ÷ 8 = _____
32 ÷ 8 = _____
40 ÷ 8 = _____
48 ÷ 8 = _____
56 ÷ 8 = _____
64 ÷ 8 = _____
72 ÷ 8 = _____

2.

Divide by 9
9 ÷ 9 = _____
18 ÷ 9 = _____
27 ÷ 9 = _____
36 ÷ 9 = _____
45 ÷ 9 = _____
54 ÷ 9 = _____
63 ÷ 9 = _____
72 ÷ 9 = _____
81 ÷ 9 = _____

Write the product or quotient.

3. $5 \times 8 =$ _____

4. $32 \div 8 =$ _____

5. $7 \times 9 =$ _____

6. $21 \div 7 =$ _____

7. $28 \div 4 =$ _____

8. $4 \times 7 =$ _____

9. $7 \times 6 =$ _____

10. $6 \times 6 =$ _____

11. $48 \div 6 =$ _____

12. $30 \div 6 =$ _____

13. $7 \times 8 =$ _____

14. $24 \div 3 =$ _____

15. $7 \times 7 =$ _____

16. $45 \div 5 =$ _____

17. $56 \div 7 =$ _____

18. $4 \times 9 =$ _____

19. $7 \div 7 =$ _____

20. $54 \div 9 =$ _____

Watch the signs!

Divide by 8 and 9; multiplication and division facts practice

Divide with 1 and 0

$4 \div 4 = 1$

4 rabbits divided into **4** groups means that there is **1** rabbit in each group.

$4 \div 1 = 4$

4 rabbits divided into **1** group means that there are **4** rabbits in that group.

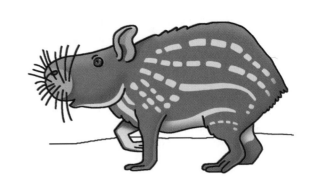

Practice the facts. Match each problem to a division rule.

Here are some division rules:

1. $3 \div 3 = \underline{\quad 1 \quad}$

2. $13 \div 1 = \underline{\qquad}$

Any number divided by 1 equals that number.
$5 \div 1 = 5$

3. $0 \div 6 = \underline{\qquad}$

4. $10 \div 10 = \underline{\qquad}$

5. $3 \div 1 = \underline{\qquad}$

6. $0 \div 15 = \underline{\qquad}$

Any non-zero number divided by itself equals 1.
$5 \div 5 = 1$

7. $8 \div 0 = \underline{\qquad}$

8. $15 \div 15 = \underline{\qquad}$

9. $7 \div 7 = \underline{\qquad}$

10. $12 \div 0 = \underline{\qquad}$

11. $0 \div 6 = \underline{\qquad}$

Zero divided by any non-zero number equals 0.
$0 \div 5 = 0$

12. $0 \div 17 = \underline{\qquad}$

13. $9 \div 1 = \underline{\qquad}$

14. $19 \div 1 = \underline{\qquad}$

15. $0 \div 0 = \underline{\qquad}$

You cannot divide by zero.
$5 \div 0 \,/\,$ cannot do

16. $20 \div 20 = \underline{\qquad}$

Practice the Division Facts

Follow the rule "Divide by 3":

$$15 \div 3 = 5$$

↑ Dividend
↑ Divisor
↑ Quotient

Divide by 3	
3	1	← 3 ÷ 3 = 1
6	2	← 6 ÷ 3 = 2
9	3	← 9 ÷ 3 = 3
12	4	← 12 ÷ 3 = 4
15	5	← 15 ÷ 3 = 5

Write the quotients and dividends to fill in each division chart.

1.

Divide by 5	
5	
10	
	3
20	
25	
	6
35	
	8
45	

2.

Divide by 7	
	1
14	
	3
28	
35	
	6
	7
56	
63	

3.

Divide by 4	
4	
	2
12	
	4
20	
24	
	7
32	
36	

4.

Divide by 8	
8	
16	
	3
32	
	5
48	
56	
	8
	9

5.

Divide by 6	
	1
	2
	3
24	
30	
	6
42	
48	
54	

6.

Divide by 9	
	1
18	
	3
36	
45	
54	
63	
	8
81	

Write Division Facts Two Ways

As you've learned, there are three parts to a division problem.
You can write a division problem two ways:

$12 \div 3 = 4$

↑   ↑   ↑
　　　　Quotient
　　Divisor
Dividend

$\begin{array}{r} 4 \leftarrow \text{Quotient} \\ 3\overline{)12} \leftarrow \text{Dividend} \end{array}$
↑
Divisor

Rewrite the division problem.

1. $32 \div 4 = 8$ 　　2. $18 \div 2 = 9$

3. $28 \div 7 = 4$　　4. $48 \div 6 = 8$

Complete the problem by finding the divisor or the quotient.

5. $18 \div 3 =$ _____

6. $\underline{}\overline{)30}$ with 6 above

7. $\underline{}\overline{)45}$ with 5 above

8. $54 \div$ _____ $= 9$

9. $56 \div 7 =$ _____

10. $7\overline{)7}$

Write the quotient.

11. $28 \div 4 =$ _____

12. $6\overline{)48}$

13. $24 \div 3 =$ _____

14. $7\overline{)49}$

15. $56 \div 8 =$ _____

16. $9\overline{)27}$

17. $1\overline{)9}$

18. $35 \div 5 =$ _____

19. $4\overline{)0}$

Multiplication and Division Facts

Write the product or quotient.

1. $\begin{array}{r} 8 \\ \times\ 2 \\ \hline \end{array}$
2. $\begin{array}{r} 9 \\ \times\ 0 \\ \hline \end{array}$
3. $\begin{array}{r} 5 \\ \times\ 9 \\ \hline \end{array}$
4. $\begin{array}{r} 4 \\ \times\ 8 \\ \hline \end{array}$
5. $\begin{array}{r} 5 \\ \times\ 6 \\ \hline \end{array}$

6. $2\overline{)14}$
7. $4\overline{)36}$
8. $6\overline{)42}$
9. $3\overline{)27}$
10. $5\overline{)40}$

11. $\begin{array}{r} 5 \\ \times\ 7 \\ \hline \end{array}$
12. $\begin{array}{r} 7 \\ \times\ 7 \\ \hline \end{array}$
13. $\begin{array}{r} 6 \\ \times\ 9 \\ \hline \end{array}$
14. $\begin{array}{r} 5 \\ \times\ 1 \\ \hline \end{array}$
15. $\begin{array}{r} 7 \\ \times\ 9 \\ \hline \end{array}$

16. $3\overline{)0}$
17. $6\overline{)54}$
18. $8\overline{)48}$
19. $7\overline{)56}$
20. $0\overline{)6}$

Write and solve a number sentence for the problem. Label your answer.

21. Carla wants to buy some animal stickers.
     She has 28 cents. Each sticker costs 7 cents.
     How many stickers can she buy?

_____

Search for the Facts

Solve the problems. Then find and circle the facts in the number search. Look across, down, and diagonally to find as many multiplication and division facts as you can.

42	6	7	7	49	9	18	1	28
45	5	9	4	36	3	3	0	4
1	30	5	6	9	9	6	4	7
7	2	3	24	3	8	2	5	9
0	5	4	63	7	9	12	18	6
8	2	35	5	6	4	27	3	63
7	3	21	9	54	6	9	15	2
32	6	8	9	8	5	40	2	9
8	4	2	81	7	3	5	6	35
4	4	16	0	56	7	8	14	7

11. $8 \times 5 =$ _____

12. $7 \times 3 =$ _____

13. $56 \div 7 =$ _____

14. $7 \times 7 =$ _____

15. $54 \div 6 =$ _____

16. $4 \times 6 =$ _____

17. $9 \times 2 =$ _____

18. $42 \div 6 =$ _____

19. $63 \div 7 =$ _____

20. $9 \times 4 =$ _____

21. $7 \times 5 =$ _____

22. $8 \times 7 =$ _____

23. $9 \times 9 =$ _____

24. $28 \div 4 =$ _____

25. $30 \div 5 =$ _____

1. $8 \times 2 =$ _____

2. $3 \times 9 =$ _____

3. $6 \times 2 =$ _____

4. $8 \div 4 =$ _____

5. $4 \times 4 =$ _____

6. $18 \div 3 =$ _____

7. $32 \div 8 =$ _____

8. $24 \div 3 =$ _____

9. $6 \times 5 =$ _____

10. $45 \div 5 =$ _____

Fact Families

If you know your multiplication facts, you can figure out related division facts.

$$\begin{array}{r} 2 \\ \times\,3 \\ \hline 6 \end{array} \quad \begin{array}{r} 3 \\ \times\,2 \\ \hline 6 \end{array}$$

$6 \div 3 = 2$

$6 \div 2 = 3$

Fill in the missing numbers for each fact family.

1.
$$\begin{array}{r} 3 \\ \times\,5 \\ \hline \Box \end{array} \quad \begin{array}{r} \Box \\ \times\,3 \\ \hline 15 \end{array}$$

$15 \div 5 = \Box$

$\Box \div 3 = 5$

2.
$$\begin{array}{r} 2 \\ \times\,\Box \\ \hline 18 \end{array} \quad \begin{array}{r} 9 \\ \times\,\Box \\ \hline 18 \end{array}$$

$\Box \div 2 = 9$

$18 \div \Box = 2$

3.
$$\begin{array}{r} 6 \\ \times\,7 \\ \hline \Box \end{array} \quad \begin{array}{r} \Box \\ \times\,6 \\ \hline 42 \end{array}$$

$42 \div 7 = \Box$

$42 \div \Box = 7$

4.
$$\begin{array}{r} \Box \\ \times\,3 \\ \hline 27 \end{array} \quad \begin{array}{r} \Box \\ \times\,9 \\ \hline 27 \end{array}$$

$\Box \div 3 = 9$

$27 \div \Box = 3$

5.
$$\begin{array}{r} 5 \\ \times\,\Box \\ \hline 30 \end{array} \quad \begin{array}{r} 6 \\ \times\,5 \\ \hline \Box \end{array}$$

$30 \div \Box = 6$

$30 \div 6 = \Box$

6.
$$\begin{array}{r} 8 \\ \times\,7 \\ \hline \Box \end{array} \quad \begin{array}{r} 7 \\ \times\,\Box \\ \hline 56 \end{array}$$

$56 \div \Box = 8$

$\Box \div 8 = 7$

Write the product. Then write related division facts.

7. $6 \times 9 = \underline{\hspace{1cm}}$

$\underline{\hspace{1cm}} \div \underline{\hspace{1cm}} = \underline{\hspace{1cm}}$

$\underline{\hspace{1cm}} \div \underline{\hspace{1cm}} = \underline{\hspace{1cm}}$

8. $9 \times 8 = \underline{\hspace{1cm}}$

$\underline{\hspace{1cm}} \div \underline{\hspace{1cm}} = \underline{\hspace{1cm}}$

$\underline{\hspace{1cm}} \div \underline{\hspace{1cm}} = \underline{\hspace{1cm}}$

9. $8 \times 0 = \underline{\hspace{1cm}}$

$\underline{\hspace{1cm}} \div \underline{\hspace{1cm}} = \underline{\hspace{1cm}}$

Fast Facts!

Watch the signs!

Time yourself. Can you do all of these problems in less than 10 minutes?

1. $3 \times 7 =$ _____
2. $35 \div 5 =$ _____
3. $18 \div 2 =$ _____
4. $8 \times 7 =$ _____
5. $21 \div 3 =$ _____
6. $9 \times 9 =$ _____
7. $1 \times 8 =$ _____
8. $48 \div 8 =$ _____
9. $9 \times 7 =$ _____
10. $6 \times 9 =$ _____
11. $28 \div 7 =$ _____
12. $7 \times 7 =$ _____

13. $30 \div 5 =$ _____
14. $8 \times 8 =$ _____
15. $3 \times 0 =$ _____
16. $4 \times 9 =$ _____
17. $54 \div 6 =$ _____
18. $6 \times 5 =$ _____
19. $27 \div 3 =$ _____
20. $5 \times 9 =$ _____
21. $64 \div 8 =$ _____
22. $1 \times 1 =$ _____
23. $8 \times 6 =$ _____
24. $81 \div 9 =$ _____

25. $8 \times 4 =$ _____
26. $42 \div 6 =$ _____
27. $72 \div 9 =$ _____
28. $6 \times 1 =$ _____
29. $5 \times 8 =$ _____
30. $7 \times 0 =$ _____
31. $7 \times 5 =$ _____
32. $35 \div 7 =$ _____
33. $6 \times 8 =$ _____
34. $24 \div 4 =$ _____
35. $56 \div 7 =$ _____
36. $3 \times 8 =$ _____

37. $9 \div 1 =$ _____
38. $4 \times 7 =$ _____
39. $45 \div 5 =$ _____
40. $2 \times 8 =$ _____
41. $1 \times 0 =$ _____
42. $32 \div 8 =$ _____
43. $2 \times 9 =$ _____
44. $56 \div 8 =$ _____
45. $9 \times 3 =$ _____
46. $42 \div 6 =$ _____
47. $6 \times 6 =$ _____
48. $54 \div 9 =$ _____

Practice multiplication and division facts

More Fast Facts!

Watch the signs!

Time yourself. Can you do all of these problems in less than 10 minutes?

1. $5 + 7 =$ _____	13. $7 \times 5 =$ _____	25. $7 - 5 =$ _____	37. $5 \div 1 =$ _____
2. $9 + 6 =$ _____	14. $7 + 0 =$ _____	26. $8 + 8 =$ _____	38. $0 \times 7 =$ _____
3. $8 \times 8 =$ _____	15. $9 \div 1 =$ _____	27. $7 + 7 =$ _____	39. $56 \div 7 =$ _____
4. $5 + 8 =$ _____	16. $17 - 8 =$ _____	28. $4 \times 9 =$ _____	40. $8 \div 8 =$ _____
5. $9 + 9 =$ _____	17. $8 \times 7 =$ _____	29. $9 + 4 =$ _____	41. $15 - 9 =$ _____
6. $14 - 5 =$ _____	18. $7 + 9 =$ _____	30. $72 \div 8 =$ _____	42. $7 \times 7 =$ _____
7. $81 \div 9 =$ _____	19. $9 + 2 =$ _____	31. $27 \div 3 =$ _____	43. $16 - 9 =$ _____
8. $6 \times 6 =$ _____	20. $45 \div 5 =$ _____	32. $7 + 8 =$ _____	44. $7 \times 9 =$ _____
9. $6 - 6 =$ _____	21. $9 \times 9 =$ _____	33. $21 \div 3 =$ _____	45. $6 + 6 =$ _____
10. $8 \times 3 =$ _____	22. $9 + 5 =$ _____	34. $63 \div 9 =$ _____	46. $64 \div 8 =$ _____
11. $54 \div 6 =$ _____	23. $8 + 3 =$ _____	35. $7 \times 8 =$ _____	47. $0 + 9 =$ _____
12. $40 \div 8 =$ _____	24. $6 \times 9 =$ _____	36. $11 - 5 =$ _____	48. $9 \times 8 =$ _____

Practice addition, subtraction, multiplication, and division facts

Multiplication Patterns

If you know a basic multiplication fact, you can find greater products. Look at the pattern:

$$3 \times 2 = 6$$
$$3 \times 20 = 60$$
$$3 \times 200 = 600$$

Think:
3 x 2 ones = 6 ones
3 x 2 tens = 6 tens
3 x 2 hundreds = 6 hundreds

Use patterns to find the products.

1. 4 x   2 = _____
    4 x 20 = _____
    4 x 200 = _____

2. 9 x   1 = _____
    9 x 10 = _____
    9 x 100 = _____

3. 3 x   5 = _____
    3 x 50 = _____
    3 x 500 = _____

4. 5 x   8 = _____
    5 x 80 = _____
    5 x 800 = _____

Find the product. Think of multiplication patterns.

5. 3 x 40 = _____

6. 5 x 20 = _____

7. 2 x 400 = _____

8. 7 x 200 = _____

9. 5 x 60 = _____

10. 6 x 70 = _____

11. 9 x 40 = _____

12. 8 x 300 = _____

13. 3 x 90 = _____

14. 4 x 700 = _____

15. 6 x 80 = _____

16. 7 x 500 = _____

Write and solve a number sentence for the problem. Label your answer.

17. There are 60 minutes in an hour. How many minutes are in 4 hours?

18. Jenna has 5 half dollars. How many cents is that? Remember, there are 100 cents in a dollar and 50 cents in a half dollar.

Estimate Products

Estimate products by **rounding** one of the factors to the **nearest ten** or **hundred**.

4 x 28
↓   ↓
4 x 30 = 120

4 x 28 is about 120.

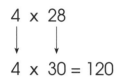

$$376 \longrightarrow 400$$
$$\underline{\times\ 7} \longrightarrow \underline{\times\ 7}$$
$$2{,}800$$

7 x 376 is about 2,800.

Round the greater number to the nearest 10 or 100.
Estimate the product.

1. 4 x 62

   4 x _____ = _____

2. 8 x 712

   8 x _____ = _____

3. 5 x 37

   5 x _____ = _____

4. 6 x 178

   6 x _____ = _____

5. 3 x 89

   3 x _____ = _____

6. 9 x 450

   9 x _____ = _____

7. 2 x 48

   _____ x _____ = _____

8. 7 x 207

   _____ x _____ = _____

9. 4 x 98

   _____ x _____ = _____

10. 55 ⟶ _____

    x 3 ⟶ _____

    _____

11. 426 ⟶ _____

    x 6 ⟶ _____

    _____

12. 75 ⟶ _____

    x 7 ⟶ _____

    _____

Write and solve a number sentence to estimate the answer. Label your estimate.

13. There are 28 grams in an ounce. About how many grams are in 8 ounces?

14. The average weight of a third grade student is 68 pounds. About how much do 4 students weigh altogether?

Multiply Two-Digit Numbers

Multiply the **ones**.
Regroup as needed.

$$\begin{array}{r} \overset{3}{1}8 \\ \times\ 4 \\ \hline 2 \end{array}$$

4 x 8 ones = 32 ones
Regroup 32 ones
to **3 tens** and **2 ones**.

Multiply the **tens**.

$$\begin{array}{r} \overset{3}{1}8 \\ \times\ 4 \\ \hline 72 \end{array}$$

4 x 1 ten = 4 tens
4 tens + 3 tens = **7 tens**
The **product** is 72.

Find the product.

1.
$$\begin{array}{r} 29 \\ \times\ 3 \\ \hline \end{array}$$

2.
$$\begin{array}{r} 12 \\ \times\ 6 \\ \hline \end{array}$$

3.
$$\begin{array}{r} 24 \\ \times\ 8 \\ \hline \end{array}$$

4.
$$\begin{array}{r} 13 \\ \times\ 4 \\ \hline \end{array}$$

5.
$$\begin{array}{r} 16 \\ \times\ 4 \\ \hline \end{array}$$

6.
$$\begin{array}{r} 33 \\ \times\ 5 \\ \hline \end{array}$$

7.
$$\begin{array}{r} 36 \\ \times\ 3 \\ \hline \end{array}$$

8.
$$\begin{array}{r} 18 \\ \times\ 2 \\ \hline \end{array}$$

9.
$$\begin{array}{r} 61 \\ \times\ 8 \\ \hline \end{array}$$

10.
$$\begin{array}{r} 52 \\ \times\ 7 \\ \hline \end{array}$$

11.
$$\begin{array}{r} 47 \\ \times\ 3 \\ \hline \end{array}$$

12.
$$\begin{array}{r} 91 \\ \times\ 9 \\ \hline \end{array}$$

13.
$$\begin{array}{r} 98 \\ \times\ 2 \\ \hline \end{array}$$

14.
$$\begin{array}{r} 34 \\ \times\ 8 \\ \hline \end{array}$$

15.
$$\begin{array}{r} 40 \\ \times\ 6 \\ \hline \end{array}$$

16.
$$\begin{array}{r} 14 \\ \times\ 7 \\ \hline \end{array}$$

Multiply two-digit numbers by one-digit numbers

Multiply Two-Digit Numbers

You might want to estimate the product before you multiply.

$$47 \longrightarrow 50$$
$$\underline{\times\ 3} \longrightarrow \underline{\times\ 3}$$
$$ 150$$

Then multiply the numbers.

$$\overset{2}{47}$$
$$\underline{\times\ 3}$$
$$141$$

The **product** of 141 is close to the estimate of 150.

To check your answer, you can use addition.

$$\overset{2}{47}$$
$$47$$
$$\underline{+\ 47}$$
$$141$$

Find the product. Use estimation or addition to check some of your answers.

1. $\begin{array}{r} 42 \\ \underline{\times\ 7} \end{array}$

2. $\begin{array}{r} 18 \\ \underline{\times\ 9} \end{array}$

3. $\begin{array}{r} 35 \\ \underline{\times\ 6} \end{array}$

4. $\begin{array}{r} 73 \\ \underline{\times\ 4} \end{array}$

5. $\begin{array}{r} 66 \\ \underline{\times\ 3} \end{array}$

6. $\begin{array}{r} 26 \\ \underline{\times\ 5} \end{array}$

7. $\begin{array}{r} 81 \\ \underline{\times\ 7} \end{array}$

8. $\begin{array}{r} 55 \\ \underline{\times\ 9} \end{array}$

9. $\begin{array}{r} 79 \\ \underline{\times\ 7} \end{array}$

10. $\begin{array}{r} 12 \\ \underline{\times\ 9} \end{array}$

11. $\begin{array}{r} 62 \\ \underline{\times\ 5} \end{array}$

12. $\begin{array}{r} 91 \\ \underline{\times\ 9} \end{array}$

13. $\begin{array}{r} 28 \\ \underline{\times\ 7} \end{array}$

14. $\begin{array}{r} 88 \\ \underline{\times\ 8} \end{array}$

15. $\begin{array}{r} 43 \\ \underline{\times\ 6} \end{array}$

16. $\begin{array}{r} 36 \\ \underline{\times\ 4} \end{array}$

Write and solve a number sentence for the problem. Label your answer.

17. Kathy has 26 rose bushes in her garden. Mandy has 3 times as many rose bushes. How many rose bushes does Mandy have?

18. Marco has 78 strawberry plants in each row of his garden. How many strawberry plants are there in 6 rows?

Multiply Three-Digit Numbers

Multiply the ones.
Regroup as needed.

$$
\begin{array}{r}
1\ 2\ \overset{3}{8} \\
\times\ \ \ \ 4 \\
\hline
2
\end{array}
$$

4 x 8 ones = 32 ones
Regroup 32 ones
to **3 tens** and **2 ones**.

Multiply the tens.
Regroup as needed.

$$
\begin{array}{r}
\overset{1}{1}\ \overset{3}{2}\ 8 \\
\times\ \ \ \ 4 \\
\hline
1\ 2
\end{array}
$$

4 x 2 tens = 8 tens
8 tens + 3 tens = 11 tens
Regroup 11 tens to
1 hundred and **1 ten**.

Multiply the hundreds.

$$
\begin{array}{r}
\overset{1}{1}\ \overset{3}{2}\ 8 \\
\times\ \ \ \ 4 \\
\hline
5\ 1\ 2
\end{array}
$$

4 x 1 hundred = 4 hundreds
4 hundreds + 1 hundred = **5 hundreds**
The **product** is **512**.

Find each product. Then look for the products in the number search.

1. $\begin{array}{r} 318 \\ \times\ \ \ 3 \\ \hline \end{array}$

2. $\begin{array}{r} 164 \\ \times\ \ \ 5 \\ \hline \end{array}$

3. $\begin{array}{r} 408 \\ \times\ \ \ 6 \\ \hline \end{array}$

4. $\begin{array}{r} 237 \\ \times\ \ \ 8 \\ \hline \end{array}$

5. $\begin{array}{r} 128 \\ \times\ \ \ 2 \\ \hline \end{array}$

6. $\begin{array}{r} 333 \\ \times\ \ \ 7 \\ \hline \end{array}$

7. $\begin{array}{r} 350 \\ \times\ \ \ 2 \\ \hline \end{array}$

8. $\begin{array}{r} 508 \\ \times\ \ \ 4 \\ \hline \end{array}$

9. $\begin{array}{r} 143 \\ \times\ \ \ 6 \\ \hline \end{array}$

8	2	8	5	8	7	9
5	2	7	1	2	1	3
0	1	0	3	8	5	2
2	3	0	4	4	9	5
8	2	4	4	2	5	6
0	2	3	3	1	4	7

Multiply Three-Digit Numbers

You might want to estimate the product before you multiply.

$$193 \longrightarrow 200$$
$$\underline{\times\ 4} \longrightarrow \underline{\times\ 4}$$
$$800$$

Then multiply the numbers.

$$\overset{3\ 1}{193}$$
$$\underline{\times\ 4}$$
$$772$$

The **product** of 772 is close to the estimate of 800.

To check your answer, you can use addition.

$$\overset{3\ 1}{193}$$
$$193$$
$$193$$
$$\underline{+193}$$
$$772$$

Estimate the product first. Then find the product.

1. Estimate: _____
   431
   x   7

2. Estimate: _____
   189
   x   6

3. Estimate: _____
   703
   x   9

4. Estimate: _____
   444
   x   5

5. Estimate: _____
   750
   x   4

6. Estimate: _____
   279
   x   3

7. Estimate: _____
   815
   x   7

8. Estimate: _____
   387
   x   2

9. Estimate: _____
   567
   x   4

Solve the problem.

10. Jim used a calculator to multiply 423 x 6.
    He got an answer of 258. Is his answer correct?
    If not, what mistake did Jim make?

_____

_____

Division Patterns

If you know a basic division fact, you can find greater quotients. Look at the pattern:

$$8 \div 2 = 4$$
$$80 \div 2 = 40$$
$$800 \div 2 = 400$$

Think:
8 ones $\div$ 2 = 4 ones
8 tens $\div$ 2 = 4 tens
8 hundreds $\div$ 2 = 4 hundreds

Use patterns to find the quotients.

1. $15 \div 3 =$ _____

$150 \div 3 =$ _____

$1,500 \div 3 =$ _____

2. $36 \div 4 =$ _____

$360 \div 4 =$ _____

$3,600 \div 4 =$ _____

3. $54 \div 9 =$ _____

$540 \div 9 =$ _____

$5,400 \div 9 =$ _____

4. $72 \div 8 =$ _____

$720 \div 8 =$ _____

$7,200 \div 8 =$ _____

Find the quotient. Think of division patterns.

5. $120 \div 4 =$ _____

6. $640 \div 8 =$ _____

7. $400 \div 2 =$ _____

8. $90 \div 3 =$ _____

9. $3,600 \div 9 =$ _____

10. $250 \div 5 =$ _____

11. $320 \div 4 =$ _____

12. $2,000 \div 5 =$ _____

13. $560 \div 8 =$ _____

Write and solve a number sentence for the problem. Label your answer.

14. There are 3 feet in a yard. If a cruise ship is about 900 feet long, how many yards long is it?

15. Jake has $4.00 in nickels. How many nickels does he have? Remember, there are 100 cents in a dollar and 5 cents in a nickel.

Estimate Quotients

To **estimate** a quotient, think of a basic division fact.

Estimate: 33 ÷ 4

Think of a basic fact.
32 ÷ 4 = 8
is close to 33 ÷ 4.

The estimate for
33 ÷ 4 is about 8.

Estimate the quotient. Write the basic division fact under the problem.

1. 26 ÷ 8 is about_____.

2. 38 ÷ 9 is about_____.

_____

_____

3. 55 ÷ 6 is about_____.

4. 26 ÷ 7 is about_____.

_____

_____

5. 45 ÷ 7 is about_____.

6. 63 ÷ 8 is about_____.

_____

_____

Estimate the quotient.

7. 37 ÷ 6 _____   8. 18 ÷ 4 _____   9. 55 ÷ 8 _____

10. 23 ÷ 3 _____   11. 64 ÷ 7 _____   12. 43 ÷ 5 _____

13. 5⟌19   14. 7⟌40   15. 6⟌50   16. 8⟌75

17. 6⟌28   18. 4⟌30   19. 8⟌33   20. 7⟌60

Division with Remainders

Count the objects. Circle groups of 3.

How many objects are there? __16__

How many groups of 3 are there? __5__

How many are left over? __1__

Follow these steps to divide numbers:
1. **Divide**
2. **Multiply**
3. **Subtract**
4. **Compare**

```
      5 R1
3 ) 16
   - 15
      1   ← remainder
```

A remainder is a "left over".

Divide the dividend by the divisor.
16 ÷ 3

Multiply the divisor by the quotient.
3 × 5 = 15

Subtract 16 – 15 = 1

Compare the remainder with the divisor. 1 < 3
If the remainder is greater than the divisor, then the quotient should be greater.

Find the quotient and remainder. Use counters if needed.

1. 3) 10   2. 4) 15   3. 6) 13   4. 2) 19   5. 5) 19

6. 6) 28   7. 8) 30   8. 4) 35   9. 7) 40   10. 9) 50

11. 8) 35   12. 5) 33   13. 6) 50   14. 4) 30   15. 7) 60

16. 3) 22   17. 7) 55   18. 9) 35   19. 8) 75   20. 6) 44

Divide two-digit numbers by one-digit numbers, with remainders

More Dividing

When you divide with greater numbers, use 5 steps.
Think of basic division facts to help you find the quotient.

Follow these steps
to divide numbers:
1. **Divide**
2. **Multiply**
3. **Subtract**
4. **Compare**
5. **Bring Down**

Divide. Multiply.
Subtract. Compare.
Bring down.

$$\begin{array}{r} 2 \\ 6\overline{)140} \\ -12\downarrow \\ \hline 20 \end{array}$$

Divide:
For 14 ÷ 6, think 12 ÷ 6.
Multiply: 6 x 2 = 12
Subtract: 14 – 12 = 2
Compare: 2 < 6
Bring down the next
digit in the dividend.

Divide. Multiply.
Subtract. Compare.

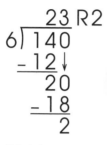

$$\begin{array}{r} 23 \text{ R2} \\ 6\overline{)140} \\ -12\downarrow \\ \hline 20 \\ -18 \\ \hline 2 \end{array}$$

Divide:
For 20 ÷ 6, think 18 ÷ 6.
Multiply: 6 x 3 = 18
Subtract: 20 – 18 = 2
Compare: 2 < 6
There are no more numbers
to bring down, so the dividing
is finished.

Multiply and add to
check your answer.

$$\begin{array}{r} 1 \\ 23 \leftarrow \text{quotient} \\ \times 6 \leftarrow \text{divisor} \\ \hline 138 \\ + 2 \leftarrow \text{remainder} \\ \hline 140 \leftarrow \text{dividend} \end{array}$$

Find the quotient. The quotient may have a remainder.

1. $3\overline{)44}$ 2. $2\overline{)72}$ 3. $4\overline{)45}$ 4. $6\overline{)90}$ 5. $5\overline{)62}$

6. $4\overline{)94}$ 7. $3\overline{)95}$ 8. $2\overline{)86}$ 9. $5\overline{)76}$ 10. $7\overline{)80}$

11. $2\overline{)125}$ 12. $3\overline{)205}$ 13. $4\overline{)156}$ 14. $5\overline{)222}$ 15. $9\overline{)234}$

Multiply to Solve Problems

To solve multiplication word problems, look for clue words like **how many** and **how much**. Multiplication clue words are similar to addition clue words.

Remember:
1. **Read**
2. **Decide**
3. **Solve**
4. **Check**

A cheetah can cover as many as **20** feet in one stride when moving at top speed. How many feet could it cover in **6** strides?

```
   20
 x  6
 120 feet
```

A cheetah can cover **120** feet in **6** strides.

Read and solve the problem. Label your answer.

1. If a gibbon can cover 12 feet in a single swing through the rain forest, how many feet can it cover in 9 swings? _____

2. An elephant in the wild needs about 400 pounds of food a day. How many pounds of food would it need in 7 days? _____

3. A grizzly bear may eat 85 pounds of fish, grasses, and leaves a day during the summer and fall months. How many pounds of food would it eat in 8 days? _____

Divide to Solve Problems

To solve division word problems, look for clue words like **share**, **how many groups**, or **how many in each group**.

Eric has **60** fish and **4** fish bowls. How many fish are in each bowl if each bowl holds the same number of fish?

$$\begin{array}{r} 15 \text{ fish} \\ 4\overline{)60} \\ -4 \\ \hline 20 \\ -20 \\ \hline 0 \end{array}$$

There are **15** fish in each fish bowl.

Read and solve the problem. Label your answer.

1. Emily has 21 birds in 7 cages. She has the same number of birds in each cage. How many birds are in each cage? _____

2. There are 9 elephants at the zoo. The zookeeper has 45 loaves of bread. The zookeeper will give the same number of loaves to each elephant. How many loaves will each elephant get? _____

3. 6 monkeys are going to share 30 bananas. How many bananas will each monkey eat? _____

4. There are 63 lions at Adventure Land Park. The lions are separated into 9 groups. How many lions are in each group? _____

Multiply or Divide to Solve Problems

Remember:
1. **Read**
2. **Decide**
3. **Solve**
4. **Check**

Mrs. Smith is going on a field trip to the zoo next Tuesday at 2 o'clock. There are **20** students in the class. Each school van can carry **5** students. How many vans are needed?

Read: What do you know? Which numbers do you use?

Decide: multiply or (divide)

Solve: $20 \div 5 = 4$ vans

Check: **5** students in each of **4** vans is equal to **20** students.

Read the problem. Circle multiply or divide. Solve the problem. Label your answer.

1. There are 24 pounds of fish to feed 8 seals. If each seal gets an equal amount of fish, how many pounds of fish do you give each seal?

   multiply or **divide** _____

2. Latisha has 15 cards. Ryan has 9 cards. Nicole has 3 times as many cards as Ryan. How many cards does Nicole have?

   multiply or **divide** _____

3. There are 6 chimpanzees at the zoo. A mother chimpanzee usually has a baby every 4 years. How many babies could she have in 28 years?

   multiply or **divide** _____

4. Shana has 48 flowers. She wants to give the same number of flowers to each of her 3 friends. How many flowers will each friend get?

   multiply or **divide** _____

Add, Subtract, Multiply, or Divide to Solve Problems

Read the problem carefully. Add, subtract, multiply, or divide to solve the problem. Label your answer.

1. The school library has 42 books about animals. 6 students are sharing the books for a project. How many books will each student have to read? _____

2. Ben read 8 books about tigers. Laura read 9 books about lions. Sam read 10 books about house cats. How many books did Ben and Sam read? _____

3. Eric has 27 animal stickers. Jose has 45 animal stickers. Adam has 19 animal stickers. How many more animal stickers does Jose have than Adam? _____

4. Emma has 14 stuffed animals. Josh has 8 stuffed animals. Hannah has 2 times as many stuffed animals as Josh. How many stuffed animals does Hannah have? _____

What I Learned about Numbers

Write the missing numbers.

1. 276, 277, _____, 279, _____, _____, 282, _____

2. 3,425, _____, 3,427, _____, 3,429, _____, _____, 3,432

Compare the numbers. Then write < or > in the ⬤.

3. 78 ⬤ 87

4. 463 ⬤ 467

5. 581 ⬤ 518

6. 607 ⬤ 670

7. 5,326 ⬤ 5,236

8. 9,803 ⬤ 9,830

Write the numbers in order from least to greatest.

9. 67, 76, 70, 66   _____, _____, _____, _____

10. 579, 597, 759, 575   _____, _____, _____, _____

11. 3,283, 3,481, 3,318, 3,287   _____, _____, _____, _____

Round the number to the nearest ten.

12. 79 _____   13. 65 _____   14. 346 _____

Round the number to the nearest hundred.

15. 509 _____   16. 828 _____   17. 450 _____

Write the number for the number written in expanded notation.

18. 8 hundreds + 4 tens + 3 ones   _____

19. 2 thousands + 5 hundreds + 8 ones   _____

What I Learned about Numbers

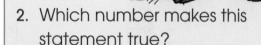

Circle the correct letter for each problem.

1. Which statement is not true?

A. 67 < 70   B. 427 > 419

C. 480 > 804   D. 4,720 > 4,719

2. Which number makes this statement true?

_____ > 3,467

A. 3,465   B. 3,461   C. 3,476   D. 3,408

3. Which number shows 65 rounded to the nearest ten?

A. 50   B. 60   C. 70   D. 100

4. Which number shows 478 rounded to the nearest hundred?

A. 400   B. 470   C. 480   D. 500

5. Which numbers come next?
566, 567, 568, ____ , ____ , ____

A. 570, 572, 574

B. 568, 569, 570

C. 569, 570, 571

D. 578, 588, 598

6. Which statement shows 609 in expanded notation?

A. 6 hundreds + 9 ones

B. 6 hundreds + 9 tens

C. 6 hundreds + 10 tens + 9 ones

D. 9 hundreds + 6 ones

7. Which numbers are in order from least to greatest?

A. 868, 876, 880, 808

B. 880, 876, 868, 808

C. 808, 880, 876, 868

D. 808, 868, 874, 880

8. Which number matches this statement in expanded notation 6,000 + 500 + 9?

A. 659   B. 6,509

C. 6,590   D. 6,000,509

What I Learned about Addition and Subtraction

Estimate the sum or difference by rounding the numbers to the nearest ten.

1. 37 + 52 _____

2. 89 – 55 _____

Estimate the sum or difference by rounding the numbers to the nearest hundred.

3. 725 – 390 _____

4. 235 + 350 _____

Find the sum or difference.

5.
```
  78
+ 43
```

6.
```
  85
– 49
```

7.
```
  483
+ 265
```

8.
```
  853
– 527
```

9.
```
  78
  63
+  9
```

10.
```
  358
+ 163
```

11.
```
  733
– 163
```

12.
```
  619
   65
+   7
```

13.
```
  4,375
– 2,632
```

14.
```
  2,468
+ 1,357
```

15. 186 + 40 + 75 = _____

16. 8 + 48 + 487 = _____

Solve the problem. Be sure to label your answer.

17. Maria collects stamps. She has 37 stamps from Mexico, 45 stamps from Canada, and 124 stamps from the United States. How many more stamps does she have from the United States than from Mexico?

18. Maria has 37 stamps from Mexico. Jason has 46 stamps from Mexico. Eric has 28 stamps from Mexico. How many stamps do Jason and Maria have from Mexico?

Review addition and subtraction facts and computation

What I Learned about Addition and Subtraction

Circle the correct letter for each problem.

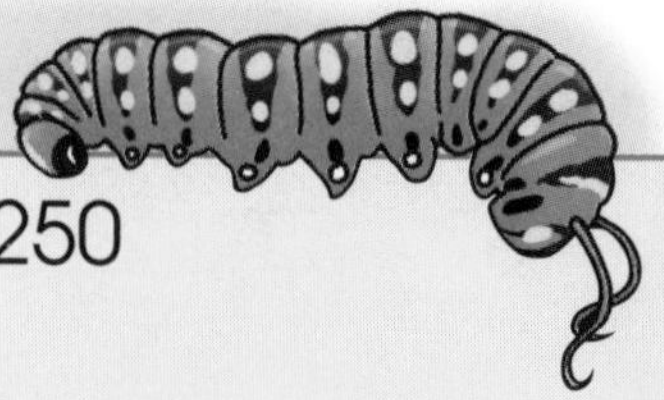

1. Estimate: 46 + 35

   A. 60

   B. 70

   C. 80

   D. 90

2. Estimate: 835 – 250

   A. 300

   B. 400

   C. 500

   D. 600

3.
$$\begin{array}{r} 90 \\ -36 \\ \hline \end{array}$$

   A. 54   B. 64

   C. 66   D. 126

4.
$$\begin{array}{r} 705 \\ -378 \\ \hline \end{array}$$

   A. 327   B. 473

   C. 1,073   D. 1,083

5. 58 + 508 + 8

   A. 566

   B. 574

   C. 1,888

   D. 6,564

6. 573 + 296

   A. 277

   B. 323

   C. 869

   D. 879

7.
$$\begin{array}{r} 5,733 \\ +1,908 \\ \hline \end{array}$$

   A. 3,825   B. 4,235

   C. 7,631   D. 7,641

8.
$$\begin{array}{r} 4,760 \\ -\ 439 \\ \hline \end{array}$$

   A. 370   B. 3,700

   C. 4,321   D. 4,439

114   Review addition and subtraction facts and computation

What I Learned about Multiplication and Division

Write the product.

1. $\begin{array}{r} 6 \\ \times 7 \\ \hline \end{array}$

2. $\begin{array}{r} 0 \\ \times 9 \\ \hline \end{array}$

3. $\begin{array}{r} 8 \\ \times 7 \\ \hline \end{array}$

4. $\begin{array}{r} 7 \\ \times 1 \\ \hline \end{array}$

5. $\begin{array}{r} 9 \\ \times 6 \\ \hline \end{array}$

6. $\begin{array}{r} 7 \\ \times 5 \\ \hline \end{array}$

7. $\begin{array}{r} 18 \\ \times 3 \\ \hline \end{array}$

8. $\begin{array}{r} 26 \\ \times 4 \\ \hline \end{array}$

9. $\begin{array}{r} 45 \\ \times 2 \\ \hline \end{array}$

Write the quotient.

10. $8 \overline{)40}$

11. $7 \overline{)49}$

12. $9 \overline{)72}$

13. $7 \overline{)63}$

14. $6 \overline{)0}$

15. $0 \overline{)5}$

16. $5 \overline{)46}$

17. $6 \overline{)62}$

18. $7 \overline{)94}$

Solve the problem. Be sure to label your answer.

19. Pete has 44 baseball cards. Nate has 2 times as many baseball cards as Pete. How many baseball cards does Nate have?

20. Jenna has 36 stickers. She wants to give the same number of stickers to 4 of her friends. How many stickers will each friend get?

What I Learned about Multiplication and Division

Circle the correct letter for each problem.

1. $8 \times 3 =$ _____

   A. 11   B. 18   C. 24   D. 32

2. $9 \times 0 =$ _____

   A. 0   B. 1   C. 9   D. 81

3. Which number makes this number sentence $8 \times$ ___ $= 48$ true?

   A. 5   B. 6   C. 7   D. 8

4. Which number makes this number sentence $7 \div$ ___ $= 7$ true?

   A. 49   B. 7   C. 1   D. 0

5. $\begin{array}{r} 36 \\ \times\ \ 3 \\ \hline \end{array}$

    A. 12   B. 33   C. 39   D. 108

6. $\begin{array}{r} 216 \\ \times\ \ \ \ 4 \\ \hline \end{array}$

    A. 54   B. 212   C. 220   D. 864

7. $6\overline{)50}$

   A. 8   B. R1   C. 8 R2   D. 9

8. $3\overline{)72}$

   A. 24   B. 2 R2   C. 20 R4   D. 216

116   Review multiplication and division facts and computation

What I Learned about Tables and Graphs

Use the table to answer questions 1-3.

1. How many maple trees were planted?

   _____

2. How many oak trees were planted?

   _____

3. How many more pine trees were planted than maple trees?

   _____

Number of Trees Planted	
Type of Tree	Number Planted
Maple	50
Oak	35
Pine	70

Use the bar graph to answer questions 4-6.

4. What is the favorite type of movie?

   _____

5. How many students like comedy?

   _____

6. How many students like space movies?

   _____

Favorite Type of Movie

Type of Movie

Cartoon
Space
Comedy

0 2 4 6 8 10 12 14 16 18 20
Number of Votes

What I Learned about Graphs

Use the bar graph to answer questions 1-4.

Favorite School Subject

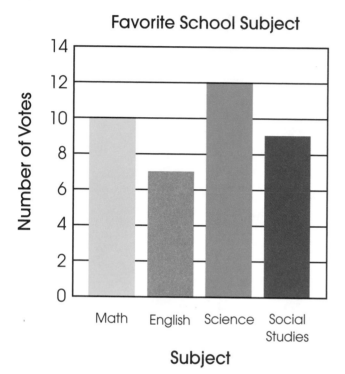

1. Which subject is the least favorite?

   A. Math   B. English

   C. Science   D. Social Studies

2. How many students like Science?

   A. 9   B. 10   C. 11   D. 12

3. How many students like Social Studies?

   A. 9   B. 10   C. 11   D. 12

4. Which statement is true?

   A. Math is the favorite subject.
   B. More students like Social Studies than Math.
   C. Science is the favorite subject.
   D. More students like English than Science.

Use the pictograph to answer questions 5-8.

Number of Books Read	
Name	**Books Read**
Juan	📕 📕 📕
Cindy	📕 📕 📕 📕 📕
Megan	📕 📕 📕 📖
Tina	📕 📕 📕 📕

 = 4 books

5. Who read the most books?

   A. Juan   B. Cindy

   C. Megan   D. Tina

6. How many books did Tina read?

   A. 12   B. 14   C. 16   D. 20

7. Who read 14 books?

   A. Juan   B. Cindy

   C. Megan   D. Tina

8. How many books did Juan and Cindy read in all?

   A. 12   B. 20   C. 24   D. 32

Cumulative Review

Watch the signs!

Find the sum, difference, product, or quotient.

1. $6 + 7 =$ _____

2. $36 \div 4 =$ _____

3. $17 - 9 =$ _____

4. $6 \times 7 =$ _____

5. $15 - 6 =$ _____

6. $8 \times 7 =$ _____

7. $8 + 7 =$ _____

8. $54 \div 9 =$ _____

9. $24 - 5 =$ _____

10. $7 + 9 =$ _____

11. $72 \div 9 =$ _____

12. $7 \times 9 =$ _____

13. $81 \div 9 =$ _____

14. $18 - 9 =$ _____

15. $9 + 0 =$ _____

16. $9 \div 0 =$ _____

17. $1 \times 6 =$ _____

18. $16 \div 2 =$ _____

19. $8 - 1 =$ _____

20. $8 \times 1 =$ _____

Find the sum, difference, product, or quotient.

21.
$$\begin{array}{r} 28 \\ + 36 \\ \hline \end{array}$$

22.
$$\begin{array}{r} 93 \\ - 45 \\ \hline \end{array}$$

23.
$$\begin{array}{r} 457 \\ + 103 \\ \hline \end{array}$$

24.
$$\begin{array}{r} 602 \\ - 187 \\ \hline \end{array}$$

25.
$$\begin{array}{r} 5,045 \\ - 366 \\ \hline \end{array}$$

26.
$$\begin{array}{r} 4,004 \\ - 1,357 \\ \hline \end{array}$$

27.
$$\begin{array}{r} 777 \\ + 888 \\ \hline \end{array}$$

28.
$$\begin{array}{r} 7,654 \\ - 2,345 \\ \hline \end{array}$$

29.
$$\begin{array}{r} 37 \\ \times 4 \\ \hline \end{array}$$

30. $3\overline{)78}$

31.
$$\begin{array}{r} 53 \\ \times 9 \\ \hline \end{array}$$

32. $4\overline{)35}$

33. $5\overline{)86}$

34.
$$\begin{array}{r} 359 \\ \times 4 \\ \hline \end{array}$$

35. $4\overline{)156}$

36.
$$\begin{array}{r} 709 \\ \times 6 \\ \hline \end{array}$$

Answer Key

Page 1

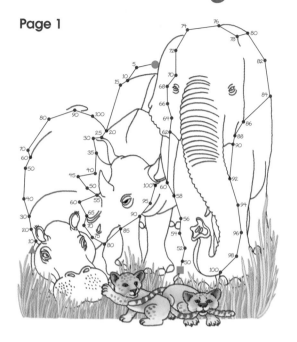

Page 2

1	②	3	④	⑤	⑥	7	⑧	9	⑩
11	⑫	13	⑭	⑮	⑯	17	⑱	19	⑳
21	㉒	23	㉔	㉕	㉖	27	㉘	29	㉚
31	㉜	33	㉞	㉟	㊱	37	㊳	39	㊵
41	㊷	43	㊹	㊺	㊻	47	㊽	49	㊿
51	52	53	54	55	56	57	58	59	60
61	62	63	64	65	66	67	68	69	70
71	72	73	74	75	76	77	78	79	80
81	82	83	84	85	86	87	88	89	90
91	92	93	94	95	96	97	98	99	100

Challenge: A number is even if it is divisible by two.

Page 3

1. 38 < 40
2. 53 > 43
3. 70 > 61
4. 45 < 54
5. <
6. >
7. >
8. >
9. <
10. >

Page 4

1. 41, 42, <u>43</u>, 44, <u>45</u>, <u>46</u>, 47, <u>48</u>, <u>49</u>, 50
2. 87, <u>88</u>, 89, <u>90</u>, 91, <u>92</u>, <u>93</u>, 94, <u>95</u>, 96
3. 66, <u>67</u>, <u>68</u>, 69, <u>70</u>, <u>71</u>, 72, <u>73</u>, 74, <u>75</u>
4. <u>73</u>, 74, <u>75</u>, <u>76</u>, 77, <u>78</u>, 79, <u>80</u>, 81, <u>82</u>
5. <u>36</u>, <u>37</u>, 38, <u>39</u>, <u>40</u>, 41, <u>42</u>, <u>43</u>, 44, <u>45</u>
6. 19, 21, 36, 47
7. 33, 56, 65, 76
8. 17, 32, 46, 59
9. 19, 26, 39, 89
10. 37, 63, 67, 73

Page 5

1. 2, 7, 27, twenty-seven
2. 4, 9, 49, forty-nine
3. 5, 0, 50, fifty
4. 3, 2, 32, thirty-two

Page 6

1. 12　2. 16
3. 50　4. 47
5. 11　6. 15
7. eighteen
8. seventy
9. fourteen
10. thirty-eight
11. fifty-six
12. seventeen
13. thirteen
14. ninety-three
15. sixty
16. nineteen
17. twenty-nine
18. sixty-eight

Page 7

1. 1st, 2nd, 3rd, 4th, 5th, 6th
2. seventh, eighth, ninth, tenth
3. 4th; 7th
4. 7
5. Ilsa
Challenge: Fran

Page 8

1. 15th
2. 5th
3. 52nd
4. 50th
5. 34th
6. 63rd
7. eleventh
8. nineteenth
9. thirty-first
10. forty-third
11. twenty-ninth
12. ninety-fifth
13. 11
14. 47th
15. 59th
16. 33rd

Page 9

1. 7, 2, 5, 7
2. 6, 9, 6, 3
3. 9, 5, 4, 9
4. 0, 6, 6, 0
5. 13, 7, 6, 13
6. 5, 13, 8, 8
7. 16, 9, 7, 16
8. 8, 12, 8, 4

Page 10

1. 6 + 8 = 14
   8 + 6 = 14
   14 − 6 = 8
   14 − 8 = 6

2. 4 + 9 = 13
   9 + 4 = 13
   13 − 4 = 9
   13 − 9 = 4

3. 7 + 8 = 15
   8 + 7 = 15
   15 − 7 = 8
   15 − 8 = 7

4. 5 + 7 = 12
   7 + 5 = 12
   12 − 5 = 7
   12 − 7 = 5

5. 5 + 9 = 14
   9 + 5 = 14
   14 − 5 = 9
   14 − 9 = 5

6. 8 + 9 = 17
   9 + 8 = 17
   17 − 8 = 9
   17 − 9 = 8

7. 6 + 9 = 15
   9 + 6 = 15
   15 − 6 = 9
   15 − 9 = 6

8. 9 + 0 = 9
   0 + 9 = 9
   9 − 9 = 0
   9 − 0 = 9

9. 7 + 7 = 14
   14 − 7 = 7

Page 11

1. 7　　2. 4　　3. 8　　4. 13
5. 9　　6. 11　7. 8　　8. 14
9. 0　　10. 7　11. 9　12. 7
13. 4　14. 13　15. 5　16. 7
17. 7　18. 11　19. 12　20. 7
21. 15　22. 6　23. 8　24. 8
25. 10　26. 6　27. 14　28. 6
29. 12　30. 5　31. 9　32. 16
33. 9　34. 17　35. 14　36. 8
37. 6　38. 11　39. 16　40. 15
41. 9　42. 9　43. 18　44. 6
45. 10　46. 6　47. 9　48. 14

Answer Key

Page 12

1. 15 2. 15 3. 19
4. 15 5. 17 6. 17
7. 13 8. 19 9. 12
10. 18 11. 17 12. 17
13. 12 14. 19 15. 7
16. 0 17. 0 18. 1

Page 13

9	2		7	5		6	5
6			4			3	3
		7	6		9	2	
	4	3		0		9	1
8			9		6		
3	3		5		5	1	

Page 14

1. 59 2. 55 3. 24
4. 89 5. 25 6. 58
7. 44 8. 59 9. 99
10. 82 11. 54 12. 104
13. 188 14. 108 15. 117
16. 83 17. 99 18. 76

Page 15

1. 43 2. 15 3. 39 4. 61
5. 1 6. 45 7. 8 8. 42
9. 49 10. 38 11. 49 12. 9
13. 55 14. 36 15. 27 16. 65

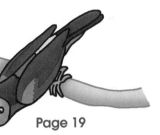

Page 16

90, 65, 51, 46, 60
45, 9, 50, 76, 75
95, 98, 56, 99, 90
46, 45, 76, 90
AFRICAN BUSH ELEPHANT

Page 17

1. 76 2. 62 3. 61 4. 18
5. 88 6. 36 7. 80 8. 53
9. 96 10. 77 11. 73 12. 65
13. 58 14. 8 15. 81 16. 8
17. 80 18. 92 19. 46 20. 42

Page 18

1. (add) 86 shells
2. (subtract) 18 shells
3. (add) 60 starfish
4. (subtract) 8 starfish

Page 19

1. 30 2. 90 3. 20 4. 60
5. 60 6. 30 7. 40 8. 80
9. 30 10. 40 11. 60 12. 30
13. 60 14. 90 15. 20 16. 50
17. 30 18. 40 19. 40 20. 70
21. 20 22. 10 23. 90 24. 80

Page 20

1. 20 + 20 = 40   2. 70 – 20 = 50
3. 80 – 50 = 30   4. 50 + 30 = 80
5. 90   6. 50   7. 10
8. 70   9. 90   10. 70

Page 21

1. 3 hundreds 7 tens 8 ones
   300 + 70 + 8   378
2. 1 hundred 9 tens 6 ones
   100 + 90 + 6   196
3. 6 hundreds 7 tens 0 ones
   600 + 70 + 0   670
4. 5 hundreds 0 tens 9 ones
   500 + 0 + 9   509

Page 22

1. 7 hundreds + 4 tens + 9 ones
2. 5 hundreds + 1 ten + 4 ones
3. 9 hundreds + 3 tens + 0 ones
4. 3 hundreds + 9 tens + 8 ones
5. 6 hundreds + 0 tens + 7 ones
6. 500 + 60 + 2
7. 900 + 50 + 3
8. 300 + 70 + 0
9. 600 + 10 + 7
10. 100 + 0 + 9

Page 23

1. 5 hundreds + 9 tens + 2 ones
   five hundred ninety-two
2. 1 hundred + 6 ones
   (or 1 hundred + 0 tens + 6 ones)
   one hundred six
3. 8 hundreds + 2 tens
   (or 8 hundreds + 2 tens + 0 ones)
   eight hundred twenty
4. three hundred seventy-two
5. one hundred eighty-nine
6. six hundred one
7. seven hundred fifteen
8. two hundred eighty
9. 306   10. 919
11. 482   12. 197
13. 550   14. 812

Page 24

1. 4 (5) 3
2. (7) 4 6
3. 1 6 (8)
4. (3) 9 1
5. 2 (1) 0
6. 7 6 (5)
7. 347
8. 605
9. 819
10. 725
11. 406
12. 345
Challenge:
469, 496,
649, 694,
946, 964

Page 25

1. 314 < 413
2. 364 > 264
3. 251 > 249
4. 204 < 240
5. <
6. >
7. >
8. >
9. <
10. <

Page 26

1. 111, <u>112</u>, 113, <u>114</u>, <u>115</u>, 116, <u>117</u>, <u>118</u>, 119, <u>120</u>
2. 307, <u>308</u>, 309, <u>310</u>, 311, <u>312</u>, <u>313</u>, 314, <u>315</u>, 316
3. 555, <u>556</u>, <u>557</u>, 558, <u>559</u>, <u>560</u>, 561, <u>562</u>, 563, <u>564</u>
4. 710, 720, <u>730</u>, 740, <u>750</u>, 760, <u>770</u>, <u>780</u>, 790, <u>800</u>
5. 872, 874, <u>876</u>, 878, <u>880</u>, 882, <u>884</u>, 886, 888, <u>890</u>
6. 319, 351, 721, 976
7. 572, 711, 897, 999
8. 237, 700, 702, 724
9. 418, 788, 808, 896
10. 381, 789, 813, 987

Answer Key

Page 27

Page 28

1. 159, 195
2. 159, 195, 519, 591
3. 348, 384, 438
4. 256, 265, 526
5. 367, 376, 637, 673
6. 456, 465, 546, 564, 645

Page 29

1. 500 2. 700 3. 600
4. 300 5. 800 6. 200
7. 500 8. 400 9. 800
10. 300 11. 600 12. 200
13. 300 14. 600 15. 600
16. 400 17. 500 18. 400
19. 140 20. 250 21. 670
22. 470 23. 490 24. 560

Page 30

1. 700 + 200 = 900
2. 700 − 100 = 600
3. 500 − 100 = 400
4. 500 + 300 = 800
5. 600   6. 600
7. 200   8. 800
9. 900   10. 900

Page 31

1. 800 2. 750 3. 621 4. 400
5. 918 6. 900 7. 834 8. 910
9. 862 10. 600 11. 700 12. 820
13. 897 14. 850 15. 835 16. 800

Page 32

1. 659 2. 588 3. 492 4. 568
5. 870 6. 595 7. 244 8. 816
9. 374 10. 437 11. 399 12. 912
13. 837 14. 873 15. 986 16. 506
17. 861 18. 935

Page 33

1. 112 2. 131
3. 210 4. 207
5. 148 6. 76
7. 542 8. 62
9. 105 10. 207
11. 745 12. 321
13. 45 14. 305
15. 550 16. 235

Page 34

1. 178 2. 307
3. 195 4. 225
5. 274 6. 49
7. 349 8. 401
9. 349 10. 34
11. 7 12. 198
13. 266 14. 37
15. 15 16. 95

Page 35

785, 700, 518, 318, 888
685, 885, 418, 585, 618
800, 785, 700, 318, 685
885, 418, 618
SALTWATER CROCODILE

Page 36

5	3	9		2	3	1
4		0		1	0	4
6	2	9		6	5	1
	1		7			
9	2		0		3	8
5		5	6	7		

Page 37

1. 132 + 78 = 210 cards
2. 304 − 257 = 47 marbles
3. She has more buttons with 2 holes.
   415 − 229 = 186 buttons
4. 45 + 28 + 9 + 13 = 95 stamps
5. 179 + 301 + 98 = 578 cans
6. 800 − 578 = 222 cans

Page 38

1. 392 − 158 = 234 pages
2. 500 − 347 = 153 pieces
3. 173 + 68 = 241 pictures
4. 512 − 309 = 203 miles
5. 365 − 147 = 218 days
6. 351 − 76 = 275 stop signs

Page 39

1. 152 + 154 = 306 miles
2. 88 + 95 + 176 = 359 miles
3. Wichita, 192 − 176 = 16 miles
4. 93 + 152 + 154 = 399 miles
5. Kansas City to Dodge City is 346 miles. Kansas City to Oakley is 359 miles.
   359 − 346 = 13 miles
6. 150 + 119 = 269 miles going through Great Bend

Page 40

1. 466 − 445 = 21 miles
2. 140 + 245 = 385 miles
3. 164 + 175 = 339 miles
4. Reno to Wells is 339 miles. Reno to Ely is 435 miles.
   435 − 339 = 96 miles
5. 164 + 175 + 140 + 245 + 445 = 1,169 miles

Page 41

1. 17 children
2. 23 children
3. bananas
4. grapes
5. 23 + 19 = 42 children
6. 28 − 17 = 11 children
7. 20 + 30 + 20 + 20 = 90 children

Page 42

1. 18 children
2. 22 children
3. 26 children
4. peas
5. carrots
6. corn
7. 20 + 26 = 46 children

Page 43

1. 27 children
2. 5, 10, 15, 20, 25, 26, 27
3. 22 children
4. 34 children
5. 20 children
6. cookies
7. 103 children

Answer Key

Page 44

1. 34 cups
2. 21 cups
3. 39 cups
4. 17 cups
5. 94 cups (from noon to 6:00 p.m.)
6. Two answers are acceptable: (A) From noon to 2:00 p.m. since this time period had the most sales. (B) From noon to 4:00 p.m. because sales were in the 30s for these two early afternoon time periods.

Page 45

1.

Button Collection		
Color	Tally	Total
Blue	‖‖‖ ‖‖‖ ‖‖‖ ‖‖‖ ‖‖‖	25
Green	‖‖‖ ‖‖‖ ‖‖‖ ‖‖	17
Red	‖‖‖ ‖‖‖ ‖‖‖ ‖‖‖ ‖‖‖ ‖‖‖ ‖‖	32

2. 17 green buttons
3. 25 blue buttons
4. red
5. green
6. 32 – 17 = 15 red buttons

Page 46

1.

Hat Collection		
Type of Hat	Tally	Total
Baseball Cap	‖‖‖ ‖‖‖ ‖‖‖ ‖‖‖ ‖‖‖ ‖‖‖ ‖‖‖	35
Cowboy Hat	‖‖‖ ‖‖‖ ‖‖‖ ‖	16
Stocking Cap	‖‖‖ ‖‖‖ ‖‖‖ ‖‖‖ ‖‖	22

2. 22 stocking caps
3. 16 cowboy hats
4. baseball caps
5. baseball caps, 35 – 16 = 19 baseball caps
6. 35 + 16 + 22 = 73 caps & hats

Page 47

1. 4 students
2. 5 students
3. 3 students
4. 11; 11 is the most common age for students in this choir.
5. 5; By subtracting 7 from 12.
6. 21 students
7. 7 students

Page 48

1. 4 students
2. 5 students
3. 52 inches
4. 7 inches
5. 8 students
6. 7 students
7. 50 inches, 52 inches, 53 inches, or 54 inches
8. 27 students
9. Most of the students are 52 inches tall or taller.

Page 49

1. 10 students
2. 32 students
3. 6 students
4. dog; 36 students
5. 6 + 10 = 16 students

Page 50

1.

Favorite Books	
Type of Book	Number of Votes
Adventure	📖 📖 📖 📖 📖
Biography	📖 📖 📖 📖 📖
Mystery	📖 📖
Science Fiction	📖 📖 📖

2. 2 symbols. If 1 symbol stands for 5 votes, then 2 symbols stand for 10 votes.
3. 4 symbols
4. Adventure; Answers may vary. Sample: The pictograph because the symbols clearly show which type has more votes.

Page 51

1. Brad; There are the most symbols after his name.
2. 10 baseballs
3. 13 baseballs
4. 8 baseballs
5. 10 + 13 = 23 baseballs
6. 14 – 8 = 6 baseballs

Page 52

1. 10, 5
2. 40 feet
3. 30 feet
4. Roger; 45 feet
5. 45 – 35 = 10 feet
6. 5 whole symbols and a half symbol

Page 53

1. 6 people
2. 12 people
3. 14 people
4. 18 people
5. hound
6. 6 + 14 = 20 people
7. 18 – 6 = 12 people

Page 54

1. 10 pounds
2. 20 pounds
3. 35 pounds; The top of the bar is at the line between 30 and 40.
4. 55 pounds
5. terrier, poodle, bulldog, collie
6. 20 + 35 = 55 pounds
7. 55 – 10 = 45 pounds

Page 55

1. 6 Siamese cats
2. 9 Persian cats; The bar ends halfway between 8 and 10.
3. Siberian; 17 Siberian cats
4. 12 Maine Coons
5. 17 – 6 = 11 Siberian cats

Page 56

1. 55 dogs
2. 40 birds
3. dogs
4. 10 cats; The top of the bar is at the 10 marker.
5. "Other" may include animals such as fish, rabbits, or turtles; 20 pets
6. 55 – 40 = 15 dogs
7. 10 + 55 = 65 cats and dogs
8. 40 + 10 + 55 + 20 = 125 pets

Page 57

1. true
2. true
3. true
4. false
5. true
6. true
7. false
8. true
9. false
10. true

Page 58

1. false
2. true
3. true
4. true
5. false
6. true
7. true
8. false
9. true
10. true

Answer Key

Page 59

1. 53 + 15 = 68 tickets
2. 40 – 15 = 25 tickets
3. 53 + 56 + 45 = 154 tickets
4. 22 + 40 = 62 tickets
5. 53 + 56 + 45 + 15 + 22 + 40 = 231 tickets
6. Sunday, 85 – 78 = 7 tickets

Page 60

1. 405 + 428 = 833 students
2. 430 – 395 = 35 boys
3. 400 + 400 = 800 students
4. 378 + 430 + 389 = 1,197 boys
5. 428 + 395 = 823 girls
6. Washington Elementary

Page 61

1. 3 thousands 1 hundred
   8 tens 5 ones
   3,000 + 100 + 80 + 5   3,185
2. 4 thousands 2 hundreds
   0 tens 7 ones
   4,000 + 200 + 0 + 7   4,207

Challenge: 9,631
Super Challenge:
1,369; 1,396; 1,639; 1,693;
1,936; 1,963; 3,169; 3,196;
3,619; 3,691; 3,916; 3,961;
6,139; 6,193; 6,319; 6,391;
6,913; 6,931; 9,136; 9,163;
9,316; 9,361; 9,613; 9,631

Page 62

1. ones
2. hundreds
3. thousands
4. thousands
5. tens
6. ones
7. 8, 1 9①
8. ④2 7 5
9. 1,②4 3
10. 9, 4⑦0
11. ⑤4 3 7
12. 9,⑦5 1

Page 63

2	6	8		3	9	7
9		4	7	8	0	3
5		3	3	3	3	9
9	0	3	5		6	2	2
			4		5	
6	7	8		5	3	9	0
8	1	2	6		1	9	0
5		2	5	5	0	

Page 64

1. >, thousands
2. <, hundreds
3. >, ones
4. <, tens
5. <, tens
6. >, thousands
7. >, tens
8. 675; 6,075; 6,507; 6,705
9. 987; 4,279; 4,297; 7,942
10. 56; 506; 6,052; 6,502

Page 65

1. 3,000 2. 7,000 3. 4,000
4. 2,000 5. 8,000 6. 5,000
7. 2,000 8. 8,000 9. 4,000
10. 3,000 11. 6,000 12. 5,000
13. 3,000 14. 6,000 15. 9,000
16. 4,000 17. 7,000 18. 7,000
19. 1,600 20. 4,700 21. 2,700
22. 3,700 23. 6,600 24. 5,600

Page 66

1. 6,000 + 4,000 = 10,000
2. 8,000 – 1,000 = 7,000
3. 3,000 – 2,000 = 1,000
4. 3,000 + 2,000 = 5,000
5. 6,000
6. 6,000
7. 2,000
8. 6,000
9. 10,000
10. 5,000

Page 67

1. 5,863 2. 6,385 3. 5,813
4. 9,022 5. 9,004 6. 8,106
7. 6,683 8. 8,852 9. 7,932
10. 8,113 11. 7,621 12. 8,173

Page 68

1. 1,084 2. 3,074 3. 294
4. 1,103 5. 1,855 6. 2,301
7. 2,722 8. 4,073 9. 2,404
10. 3,116 11. 3,740 12. 2,207

Page 69

1. 1,478 2. 3,407
3. 1,864 4. 4,225
5. 2,754 6. 499
7. 3,051 8. 5,528
9. 6,712 10. 4,534
11. 107 12. 5,994
13. 4,966 14. 6,404
15. 3,917 16. 1,995

Page 70

4	0	8		6	8	4
1		1	8		8	
2	0	4		6	5	6
		3	9	4		0
7	2		4	3	0	6
1	9	8		2		

Page 71

1. 1,500 – 793 = 707 pieces
2. U.S.–Canadian border, 3,987 – 1,933 = 2,054 miles
3. Willis Tower, 1,450 – 1,250 = 200 feet
4. 2007 – 1949 = 58 years old
5. 8,765 + 1,234 = 9,999
6. 8,765 – 1,234 = 7,531

Page 72

1. 3,003 – 1,786 = 1,217 people
2. 1,786 + 2,467 + 3,095 + 798 = 8,146 people
3. 3,095 – 2,467 = 628 people
4. 3,000 + 3,000 + 2,000 + 1,000 = 9,000 people
5. 3,003 – 1,170 = 1,833 people
6. Hondo, 3,095 – 2,286 = 809 people

Page 73

1. 2 x 4 = 8
2. 2 x 5 = 10
3. 2 x 6 = 12
4. 3 x 6 = 18
5. 2 x 8 = 16
6. 2 x 7 = 14

Answer Key

Page 74

1.	2	2.	3	3.	1	4.	0
	4		6		2		0
	6		9		3		0
	8		12		4		0
	10		15		5		0
	12		18		6		0
	14		21		7		0
	16		24		8		0
	18		27		9		0

Page 75

1.	4	2.	5	3. 20	4. 0
	8		10	5. 9	6. 20
	12		15	7. 35	8. 21
	16		20	9. 5	10. 32
	20		25	11. 18	12. 45
	24		30	13. 14	14. 10
	28		35	15. 12	16. 16
	32		40	17. 18	18. 28
	36		45		

Page 76

Answers are clockwise from the arrow.

1. 10, 16, 8, 14, 12, 18
2. 28, 32, 16, 24, 36, 20
3. 15, 25, 40, 35, 30, 45
4. 18, 24, 12, 21, 15, 27

Page 77

1.	6	2.	7	3. 3	4. 0	5. 2
	12		14	6. 24	7. 27	8. 8
	18		21	9. 9	10. 7	11. 6
	24		28	12. 6	13. 1	14. 6
	30		35			
	36		42			
	42		49			
	48		56			
	54		63			

Page 78

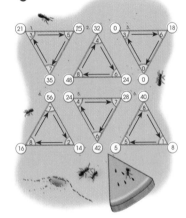

Page 79

1.	8	2.	9	0 + 9 = 9
	16		18	1 + 8 = 9
	24		27	2 + 7 = 9
	32		36	3 + 6 = 9
	40		45	4 + 5 = 9
	48		54	5 + 4 = 9
	56		63	6 + 3 = 9
	64		72	7 + 2 = 9
	72		81	8 + 1 = 9

3.

X	0	1	2	3	4	5	6	7	8	9
0	0	0	0	0	0	0	0	0	0	0
1	0	1	2	3	4	5	6	7	8	9
2	0	2	4	6	8	10	12	14	16	18
3	0	3	6	9	12	15	18	21	24	27
4	0	4	8	12	16	20	24	28	32	36
5	0	5	10	15	20	25	30	35	40	45
6	0	6	12	18	24	30	36	42	48	54
7	0	7	14	21	28	35	42	49	56	63
8	0	8	16	24	32	40	48	56	64	72
9	0	9	18	27	36	45	54	63	72	81

Page 80

1. 8, 8
2. 21, 21
3. 45, 45
4. 48, 48
5. 36, 36
6. 9, 63
7. 40, 5
8. 42, 7
9. 3, 27
10. 54, 9
11. 0, 0
12. 1, 8
13. 30, 5 x 6 = 30
14. 63, 7 x 9 = 63
15. 72, 9 x 8 = 72
16. 54, 6 x 9 = 54

Page 81

Page 81 puzzle grid:
1. 1 0
2. 2 4
3. 3 0
4. 1 2
5. 1 6
6. 3 5
7. 1 2
8. 1 8
9. 4 0
10. 2 5
11. 2 1
12. 2 4
8

Page 82

1. 18	2. 25	3. 24	4. 81
5. 21	6. 0	7. 45	8. 48
9. 24	10. 56	11. 36	12. 35
13. 7	14. 12	15. 36	16. 40
17. 54	18. 27	19. 28	20. 72
21. 63	22. 18	23. 42	24. 32
25. 24	26. 18	27. 45	28. 49
29. 32	30. 64	31. 8	32. 0
33. 48	34. 42	35. 72	36. 9
37. 0	38. 56	39. 28	40. 12
41. 63	42. 30	43. 9	44. 16
45. 36	46. 54	47. 21	48. 40

Page 83

1. 3, 12 ÷ 4 = 3
2. 5, 15 ÷ 3 = 5
3. 10, 10, 5, 10 ÷ 2 = 5
4. 12, 12, 3, 12 ÷ 4 = 3
5. 18, 6, 18 ÷ 3 = 6
6. 24, 4, 24 ÷ 6 = 4

Page 84

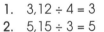

1. 4, 4
2. 5, 5
3. 7, 7
4. 6, 6
5. 1, 2, 3, 4, 5, 6, 7, 8, 9

Page 85

1. 4, 4
2. 5, 5
3. 6, 6
4. 7, 7
5. 1, 2, 3, 4, 5, 6, 7, 8, 9

Answer Key

Page 86

1. 1 2. 1 3. 2 4. 2
   2   2 5. 5 6. 3
   3   3 7. 5 8. 7
   4   4 9. 4 10. 4
   5   5 11. 5 12. 9
   6   6 13. 2 14. 2
   7   7 15. 4 16. 6
   8   8 17. 7 18. 7
   9   9

Page 87

1. 1 2. 1 3. 6 4. 7
   2   2 5. 7 6. 9
   3   3 7. 30 8. 42
   4   4 9. 7 10. 7
   5   5 11. 6 12. 6
   6   6
   7   7
   8   8
   9   9

Page 88

1. 1 2. 1 3. 40 4. 4 5. 63
   2   2 6. 3 7. 7 8. 28
   3   3 9. 42 10. 36 11. 8
   4   4 12. 5 13. 56 14. 8
   5   5 15. 49 16. 9 17. 8
   6   6 18. 36 19. 1 20. 6
   7   7
   8   8
   9   9

Page 89

1. 1
3. 0
5. 3
7. cannot do
9. 1
11. 0
13. 9
15. cannot do

Any number divided by 1 equals that number.
5 ÷ 1 = 5

Any non-zero number divided by itself equals 1.
5 ÷ 5 = 1

Zero divided by any non-zero number equals 0.
0 ÷ 5 = 0

You cannot divide by zero.
5 ÷ 0/cannot do

2. 13
4. 1
6. 0
8. 1
10. cannot do
12. 0
14. 19
16. 1

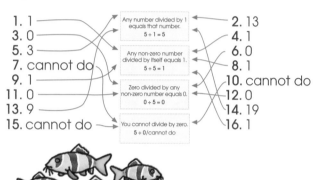

Page 90

1. Divide by 5

5	1
10	2
15	3
20	4
25	5
30	6
35	7
40	8
45	9

2. Divide by 7

7	1
14	2
21	3
28	4
35	5
42	6
49	7
56	8
63	9

3. Divide by 4

4	1
8	2
12	3
16	4
20	5
24	6
28	7
32	8
36	9

4. Divide by 8

8	1
16	2
24	3
32	4
40	5
48	6
56	7
64	8
72	9

5. Divide by 6

6	1
12	2
18	3
24	4
30	5
36	6
42	7
48	8
54	9

6. Divide by 9

9	1
18	2
27	3
36	4
45	5
54	6
63	7
72	8
81	9

Page 91

1. $4\overline{)32}$ = 8   2. $2\overline{)18}$ = 9
3. $7\overline{)28}$ = 4   4. $6\overline{)48}$ = 8
5. 6   6. 5
7. 9   8. 6
9. 8   10. 1
11. 7   12. 8   13. 8
14. 7   15. 7   16. 3
17. 9   18. 7   19. 0

Page 92

1. 16   2. 0   3. 45
4. 32   5. 30   6. 7
7. 9   8. 7   9. 9
10. 8   11. 35   12. 49
13. 54   14. 5   15. 63
16. 0   17. 9   18. 6
19. 8   20. cannot do
21. 28 ÷ 7 = 4 stickers

Page 93

1. 8 x 2 = 16   11. 8 x 5 = 40   21. 7 x 5 = 35
2. 3 x 9 = 27   12. 7 x 3 = 21   22. 8 x 7 = 56
3. 6 x 2 = 12   13. 56 ÷ 7 = 8   23. 9 x 9 = 81
4. 8 ÷ 4 = 2   14. 7 x 7 = 49   24. 28 ÷ 4 = 7
5. 4 x 4 = 16   15. 54 ÷ 6 = 9   25. 30 ÷ 5 = 6
6. 18 ÷ 3 = 6   16. 4 x 6 = 24
7. 32 ÷ 8 = 4   17. 9 x 2 = 18
8. 24 ÷ 3 = 8   18. 42 ÷ 6 = 7
9. 6 x 5 = 30   19. 63 ÷ 7 = 9
10. 45 ÷ 5 = 9   20. 9 x 4 = 36

Page 94

1. 15, 5, 3, 15
2. 9, 2, 18, 9
3. 42, 7, 6, 6
4. 9, 3, 27, 9
5. 6, 30, 5, 5
6. 56, 8, 7, 56
7. 6 x 9 = 54
   54 ÷ 6 = 9
   54 ÷ 9 = 6
8. 9 x 8 = 72
   72 ÷ 8 = 9
   72 ÷ 9 = 8
9. 8 x 0 = 0
   0 ÷ 8 = 0

Page 95

1. 21   2. 7   3. 9   4. 56
5. 7   6. 81   7. 8   8. 6
9. 63   10. 54   11. 4   12. 49
13. 6   14. 64   15. 0   16. 36
17. 9   18. 30   19. 9   20. 45
21. 8   22. 1   23. 48   24. 9
25. 32   26. 7   27. 8   28. 6
29. 40   30. 0   31. 35   32. 5
33. 48   34. 6   35. 8   36. 24
37. 9   38. 28   39. 9   40. 16
41. 0   42. 4   43. 18   44. 7
45. 27   46. 7   47. 36   48. 6

Page 96

1. 12   2. 15   3. 64   4. 13
5. 18   6. 9   7. 9   8. 36
9. 0   10. 24   11. 9   12. 5
13. 35   14. 7   15. 9   16. 9
17. 56   18. 16   19. 11   20. 9
21. 81   22. 14   23. 11   24. 54
25. 2   26. 16   27. 14   28. 36
29. 13   30. 9   31. 9   32. 15
33. 7   34. 7   35. 56   36. 6
37. 5   38. 0   39. 8   40. 1
41. 6   42. 49   43. 7   44. 63
45. 12   46. 8   47. 9   48. 72

Page 97

1. 8; 80; 800
2. 9; 90; 900
3. 15; 150; 1,500
4. 40; 400; 4,000
5. 120   6. 100
7. 800   8. 1,400
9. 300   10. 420
11. 360   12. 2,400
13. 270   14. 2,800
15. 480   16. 3,500
17. 60 x 4 = 240 minutes
18. 50 x 5 = 250 cents

Answer Key

Page 98

1. 4 x 60 = 240
2. 8 x 700 = 5,600
3. 5 x 40 = 200
4. 6 x 200 = 1,200
5. 3 x 90 = 270
6. 9 x 500 = 4,500
7. 2 x 50 = 100
8. 7 x 200 = 1,400
9. 4 x 100 = 400
10. 60 x 3 = 180
11. 400 x 6 = 2,400
12. 80 x 7 = 560
13. 30 x 8 = 240 grams
14. 70 x 4 = 280 pounds

Page 99

1. 87 2. 72 3. 192 4. 52
5. 64 6. 165 7. 108 8. 36
9. 488 10. 364 11. 141 12. 819
13. 196 14. 272 15. 240 16. 98

Page 100

1. 294 2. 162 3. 210 4. 292
5. 198 6. 130 7. 567 8. 495
9. 553 10. 108 11. 310 12. 819
13. 196 14. 704 15. 258 16. 144
17. 26 x 3 = 78 rose bushes
18. 78 x 6 = 468 strawberry plants

Page 101

1. 954 2. 820 3. 2,448
4. 1,896 5. 256 6. 2,331
7. 700 8. 2,032 9. 858

8	2	8	5	8	7	9
5	2	7	1	2	1	3
0	1	0	3	8	5	9
2	3	0	4	4	9	5
8	2	4	4	2	5	6
0	2	3	3	1	4	7

Page 102

1. 2,800; 3,017
2. 1,200; 1,134
3. 6,300; 6,327
4. 2,000; 2,220
5. 3,200; 3,000
6. 900; 837
7. 5,600; 5,705
8. 800; 774
9. 2,400; 2,268
10. His answer is not correct. If he had made an estimate first, he would know that the product should be close to 400 x 6, or 2,400. He may not have pressed enough keys because 43 x 6 = 258. 423 x 6 = 2,538, which is close to the estimate of 2,400.

Page 103

1. 5, 50, 500 2. 9, 90, 900
3. 6, 60, 600 4. 9, 90, 900
5. 30 6. 80 7. 200
8. 30 9. 400 10. 50
11. 80 12. 400 13. 70
14. 900 ÷ 3 = 300 yards
15. 400 ÷ 5 = 80 nickels

Page 104

1. 3, 24 ÷ 8 = 3
2. 4, 36 ÷ 9 = 4
3. 9, 54 ÷ 6 = 9
4. 4, 28 ÷ 7 = 4
5. 6, 42 ÷ 7 = 6
6. 8, 64 ÷ 8 = 8
7. 6 8. 4 or 5
9. 7 10. 8
11. 9 12. 9
13. 4 14. 6
15. 8 16. 9
17. 5 18. 7 or 8
19. 4 20. 9

Page 105

1. 3 R1 2. 3 R3 3. 2 R1
4. 9 R1 5. 3 R4 6. 4 R4
7. 3 R6 8. 8 R3 9. 5 R5
10. 5 R5 11. 4 R3 12. 6 R3
13. 8 R2 14. 7 R2 15. 8 R4
16. 7 R1 17. 7 R6 18. 3 R8
19. 9 R3 20. 7 R2

Page 106

1. 14 R2 2. 36 3. 11 R1
4. 15 5. 12 R2 6. 23 R2
7. 31 R2 8. 43 9. 15 R1
10. 11 R3 11. 62 R1 12. 68 R1
13. 39 14. 44 R2 15. 26

Page 107

1. 108 feet
2. 2,800 pounds
3. 680 pounds

Page 108

1. 3 birds
2. 5 loaves
3. 5 bananas
4. 7 lions

Page 109

1. (divide) 3 pounds
2. (multiply) 27 cards
3. (divide) 7 babies
4. (divide) 16 flowers

Page 110

1. 7 books
2. 18 books
3. 26 stickers
4. 16 stuffed animals

Page 111

1. 276, 277, 278, 279, 280, 281, 282, 283
2. 3,425; 3,426; 3,427; 3,428; 3,429; 3,430; 3,431; 3,432
3. < 4. < 5. > 6. < 7. > 8. <
9. 66, 67, 70, 76
10. 575, 579, 597, 759
11. 3,283; 3,287; 3,318; 3,481
12. 80 13. 70 14. 350 15. 500
16. 800 17. 500 18. 843 19. 2,508

Page 112

1. C 2. C
3. C 4. D
5. C 6. A
7. D 8. B

Page 113

1. 90 2. 30
3. 300 4. 600
5. 121 6. 36
7. 748 8. 326
9. 150 10. 521
11. 570 12. 691
13. 1,743 14. 3,825
15. 301 16. 543
17. 87 stamps
18. 83 stamps

Page 114

1. D 2. C
3. A 4. A
5. B 6. C
7. D 8. C

Page 115

1. 42 2. 0
3. 56 4. 7
5. 54 6. 35
7. 54 8. 104
9. 90 10. 5
11. 7 12. 8
13. 9 14. 0
15. cannot do
16. 9 R1 17. 10 R2
18. 13 R3
19. 88 baseball cards
20. 9 stickers

Page 116

1. C 2. A
3. B 4. C
5. D 6. D
7. C 8. A

Page 117

1. 50 maple trees
2. 35 oak trees
3. 20 pine trees
4. Comedy
5. 16 students
6. 7 students

Page 118

1. B 2. D
3. A 4. C
5. B 6. C
7. C 8. D

Page 119

1. 13 2. 9 3. 8 4. 42
5. 9 6. 56 7. 15 8. 6
9. 19 10. 16 11. 8 12. 63
13. 9 14. 9 15. 9 16. cannot do
17. 6 18. 8 19. 7 20. 8
21. 64 22. 48 23. 560 24. 415
25. 4,679 26. 2,647 27. 1,665 28. 5,309
29. 148 30. 26 31. 477 32. 8 R3
33. 17 R1 34. 1,436 35. 39 36. 4,254

Answer key 127

Award

Congratulations!

_____

NAME

finished
Math 3

from
School Zone Interactive.

          On-Track Software & Workbook Math Basics 3 09303